CAPTIVE

HUMANS

CAPTIVE

HUMANS

TRUE CRIME CASES
OF PEOPLE HELD CAPTIVE

DAVID PHOEBE

A special thanks to Richard Ellis and Rachael Gregory.

National Library of Australia Cataloguing-in-Publication entry

   Author: Phoebe, David.
   Title: Captive humans : true crime cases of people held
        captive / David Phoebe.
   ISBN: 9780987374608 (paperback)
   Subjects: Kidnapping.
             Kidnapping victims.
             Captivity.
   Dewey Number: 364.154

Cover design by David Phoebe.

This book is dedicated to:

Everyone who feels captive
in their own lives,
Those who are coping with violence,
And those who are just getting by.

Further information available at

www.captivehumans.com

INTRODUCTION

Ever wondered what leads someone to hold another human captive? Why would they do it? What urges drive a person to take another as a possession? What is the motivation to enact one of the most heinous crimes imaginable? Who commits these crimes?

Every so often we are presented with another shocking case, all by their very nature are incredibly complex. Without following these cases closely it is easy to get lost in the speculation, confused with the detail, or left wondering when loose ends are never tied off as the media moves onto the next story.

Some cases are well known, like that of Elisabeth Fritzl, Jaycee Dugard, and Natascha Kampusch. Josef Fritzl held his daughter in a basement dungeon for 24 years, creating an incestuous family, living two lives. But, there are many other cases that almost evade the public eye. While Elisabeth's story is traumatic, she is far from alone. David Bisson spent his childhood locked in a cupboard, while his mother denied his existence. Under the ice covered grounds of Russia, a copycat kidnapper aimed to recreate Alexander Komin's vision of an underground city of slaves. James Jamelske got away with holding five women captive over 15 years, before anyone would believe their stories.

Captive Humans explores true crime cases of people held captive, examining the stories in a chronological order. These cases present the facts; you can draw your own conclusions.

Come into the dark, hard places and explore the secretive world of *Captive Humans*.

CHAPTER 01

SUSAN "GENIE" WILEY

TEMPLE CITY, CALIFORNIA

- UNITED STATES.

1970

Susan Wiley is more famously known as "Genie." She suffered some of the worst child abuse recorded in the history of the United States. Held captive in a bedroom, her cruel father deprived her of all social stimulation, before she was thrust into the public spotlight, and under the gaze of researchers and academics.

LEAD UP TO CRIME

Susan's father, Clark Wiley, came from a dysfunctional background. He was teased relentlessly while growing up because he was given the same birth name as his mother, Pearl Wiley. Raised by a mother who managed a bordello, Clark discovered her with clients. His father was killed when struck by lightning.

Clark worked as an aircraft mechanic, and married Dorothy "Irene" Oglesby in 1944. He was 20 years older than his wife and he never wanted children. Clark suffered mental instability, while Irene was partially blind. Their marriage was littered with domestic violence, which would see Irene hospitalised. They would have four children, but not all would survive.

Their first child, Dorothy Irene Wiley, was born on June 2, 1948, and named after her mother. When Dorothy was around ten-weeks old, Clark wrapped the crying infant in a blanket and placed her in a dresser drawer in the garage, resulting in her death.

Their second child, Robert Clark Wiley, was born a year later on September 15, 1949. He died two days later; it was reported he choked on his own mucus. It has been suspected that Clark caused his son's death.

John Gray Wiley, their third child, was born on March 11, 1952. At four years of age he went to live with his grandmother, Pearl Martin, after mother Irene was institutionalised. At age six, Pearl took John out for an ice cream. In a hit-and-run, she was struck by a pick-up truck and killed. John returned to live with his parents. Clark blamed his son for his mother's death.

The family moved into Pearl's small two-bedroom house at 6722 North Golden West Avenue, Temple City, Los Angeles, California. (The property is located two houses from the town line — situated just inside Temple City — but is often listed with an Arcadia postal address.) Clark's mother's bedroom remained untouched, left as a shrine.

Susan M., the fourth of the Wiley children, was born on April 18, 1957.

HELD CAPTIVE

In late 1958, when Susan was 20 months old, a doctor told her father the girl was mildly retarded and should be protected from the world. Clark Wiley took this to the extreme, locking her in the remaining bedroom of the house. For years Clark slept in an armchair in the living room, with a gun on his lap, as Irene slept at the dining table, and John slept on the floor. Clark rarely allowed the family to leave and forced them to live in the darkened house, with the blinds constantly drawn.

Susan spent her time strapped to a potty chair, often overnight. She was housed in a cot, caged in with chicken wire. She was restrained in a homemade straightjacket sown by Irene, and slept tied up in a tattered sleeping bag.

When Susan made a noise she was beaten, barked or growled at by her father. Her mother, Irene, and brother, John, also suffered punishments at the hands of Clark; he often treated them violently, or threatened them with his gun collection. No one was allowed to visit or talk to Susan, who remained trapped in a dingy room, with the windows covered in foil.

Fed on a diet of pablum (a processed cereal for infants' that contains vitamin D) and soft foods, Susan never learned to chew solids. She suffered from malnutrition and her body failed to grow at an average rate.

In his armchair, Clark rested with a gun across his lap, leaving Irene and John in a constant state of fear. John attended school, keeping the family secret, avoiding gym classes because of his bruised and swollen genitalia, a result of being regularly beaten by his father with a wooden plank. Clark beat Susan with the same plank.

Susan learned only limited words, such as "stop it" and "no more," basic phrases to protest her father's atrocities.

Neighbours thought the Wiley family were "strange people who kept to themselves." Others claimed they saw the girl sitting on the porch, while most claimed to know nothing of Susan's existence.

John ran away at 18 years of age to escape his father. Irene soon did the same and fled to her mother's house with Susan. Susan had been held captive for 12 years.

RESCUE

Irene left her mother's house in Monterey Park on November 4, 1970, intending to visit the Temple City welfare office to seek blind assistance payments. However, she accidentally attended the County Department of Public Social Services, where a welfare worker noticed something wasn't right with Susan. She moved with a "bunny walk," her legs deformed from being strapped to the potty. She looked around eight years old, she could not speak, her hands extended claw-like, and she still wore diapers.

Irene Wiley applied for welfare and a worker attended her home. The worker enquired about Susan's age and discovered the girl was 13-years-old. The Los Angeles County Sheriff's Department was contacted.

On November 5, 1970, Clark and Irene Wiley were arrested and charged with the felony of wilful cruelty toward a child. Both parents were released on a $1,250 bond each.

Susan was taken to the Children's Hospital in Los Angeles. Doctors stated the lack of social contact was the reason for her apparent retardation. Doctors also noted that her bones were thin, she shuffled like an elderly person, and she had the mental capacity of an infant. Doctors estimated the time for her recovery, until normal functioning, would take around two years.

The public interest was immediate and immense. Soon hundreds of cars streamed down Golden West Avenue to catch a glimpse of the unremarkable sandy coloured house.

"I tried to run them off," said Bruce Moore, 18, friend of John Wiley. "I went out and told them, 'The road goes that way.'"

TRIAL

Clark Wiley stated he was "burning to tell the story," though he was instructed by his attorney not to say anything until the matter reached court.

On Friday, November 20, 1970, John Wiley waited outside the Temple City house to drive his father to his court hearing. John returned after the story broke. The waited on the road to capture the car departing.

A gunshot was heard.

John discovered his father's body in the living room at 8:45 a.m. He reappeared outside, stating someone had shot his father. Police confirmed Clark Wiley, 70, had shot himself in the head with a .38-calibre pistol.

Irene was arraigned and she pleaded "not guilty" to charges of felony child abuse. She was instructed to appear in court on December 4. Shortly after her hearing she was told of her husband's death. Family friends blamed the media and sightseers for the suicide, and on November 21 the *Reno Evening Gazette* ran the headline, "Curiosity seekers drive accused man to suicide."

Clark left a suicide note; there have been many claims to its contents. "The world will never understand." "John will understand." "Be a good boy, I love you." "My son John is in charge."

Judge Peter S. Smith of the Alhambra Municipal Court dismissed Irene Wiley's case in December 1970. Judge Smith reached the decision, "[There's] no question of what happened to this child." He added, "I can't see the Superior Court judge or jury, convicting this woman."

AFTERMATH

The National Institute of Mental Health sponsored Susan's care, where attempts were made to teach her to speak, walk, and socialise. She was attracted to colourful objects and classical music.

Many psychologists, doctors, academics, and researchers came to study the girl. They labelled Susan "Genie" and "The Wild Child," names which she would become famously known for. Battles between academics and linguists ensued over Susan, as warring parties sought to make a name for themselves. Special educator, Jean Butler, allegedly boasted, "I'm going to be the next Annie Sullivan." Sullivan was the teacher and companion of Helen Keller. Butler took Susan into her house, claiming the girl had been exposed to German measles, and applied to become her foster parent. She was denied.

In 1971, Doctor David Rigler fostered Susan and used her as a case study. A great deal of Susan's experiences, and many experiments on her, were recorded, but the was neither clearly defined nor organised in any significant way. Theories of linguistics were tested, and many people conducting experiments on the girl gained academic notoriety, but less care was taken to ensure Susan's long-term prospects.

In 1975 the funding for "Genie" ran out, so did much of the academic interest. The Rigler's gave up fostering Susan. She never made a full recovery.

Irene initially regained custody of Susan but it was short lived, as she found caring for the girl too strenuous. Susan passed through several foster homes where she was further abused, causing her to regress. On one occasion she was beaten for vomiting, causing her to become fearful of opening her mouth. A lawsuit launched by Irene Wiley prevented all academics having further involvement with Susan's life.

John Wiley garnered no attention from police or psychologists, and received no help to deal with the trauma. A forgotten victim. One day he left the Temple City home and drove until he eventually found himself in Urbana, Ohio. He gained employment as a house painter and handyman. His life was tragic, littered with alcohol abuse, familial problems, and a series of menial jobs. He carried a great deal of shame about Susan and rarely discussed the past. He last saw his sister in 1982, when he ventured back to Temple City to say good-bye to his past.

Irene remained in contact with her daughter, visiting

Susan where she lived in assisted living homes. Irene Wiley died in 2003.

John Wiley passed away on February 18, 2011, in Urbana, Ohio, aged 58: He never told even the closest of his new extended family about his early ordeals.

Susan resides in a small private adult care home in California. Her location remains a closely guarded secret to protect her from intrusion.

CHAPTER 02

BERNARDO RAMOS

PHILADELPHIA, PENNSYLVANIA

- UNITED STATES.

1981

For the residents living along the crime riddled streets of North Philadelphia, hardship is a way of life. However, behind the façade of an aging and dilapidated row house, in one of the cities most impoverished areas, a series of deplorable crimes were committed. For the Weston family, there really was no place like home.

LEAD UP TO CRIME

When Alice Collier died in the 1970s she left her teenage daughter, Linda Ann Weston, behind to take care of her twelve siblings. The family lived in an apartment situated near the corner of North 33rd Street and West Norris Street in Strawberry Mansion, Philadelphia. No fathers were involved in the upbringing of the children. Linda developed a domineering personality, splintered by her mother's death. She grew fearful of evil spirits and controlled her younger siblings with extreme violence.

Weston would spike her siblings Kool Aid with narcotics, as a means of keeping them in the apartment. The drugs made them easy to control and quick to overpower if they attempted to flee. One of the younger girls, Valerie, was afraid to go outside, fearing her sister's violent nature. "She used to hit me all the time."

Linda reigned over the family with a ruthless terror. She tortured her brothers and sisters with continual beatings and ordered them to complete chores, such as constant cleaning and scrubbing of the walls. She tied them up for days on end. The children became so conditioned to Linda's torment that they never challenged her, fearful for their own safety.

She forced her siblings, some as young as 11, into prostitution with older men to make her money. Weston kidnapped relatives and took advantage of mentally disabled people, often holding them at different places around Philadelphia, and at times sexually abusing them.

The Weston house was plagued by incest from when Linda was nine years old, according to the testimony of a prison chaplain. She went on to make her family members perform incest, with the aim that they would have children so she could collect the Social Security payments. She would also have sex with her brothers and sisters. Her younger brother, aged eight, refused to watch her have sex with their cousin. He was hospitalised after Linda punished him by putting him in a hot oven, causing him to suffer burns, blisters and welts.

In 1979, while in her early twenties, Linda Weston gave birth to her first child, Jean McIntosh, followed by James a year later. Joseph would arrive in 1982, with Raymond the year after, but before they were born more children were on the way to fill the already crowded household.

HELD CAPTIVE

Linda Weston's sister, Venus, 19, became pregnant by Bernardo Ramos, 25, but he refused to financially support their unborn baby. Venus Weston "was afraid he was going to go away and not come back no more."

Linda Ann Weston, 21, bashed her sister's boyfriend with a hammer and a broomstick as he attempted to leave the apartment. "You wasn't going to take care of my sister's baby," screamed Weston.

Ramos was described by prosecutors as being "possibly

mildly mentally retarded." He was much smaller than the two women, standing only 165 centimetres (5 foot, 4 inches).

Linda Weston ordered her brother, 11-year-old Alexander, to tie Ramos' hands and feet with an electrical cord and strap him to a chair. In October 1981, the sisters locked Ramos in a rat-infested closet measuring 90 centimetres by three metres (3 x 10 feet). Water dripped through the leaky ceiling, providing his only source of fluids. They let him out sporadically to use the toilet.

Ramos kicked at the door as he attempted to summon for help. Alexander tried to smuggle the captive food but Linda caught him. As punishment, she broke his toes with a hammer. He would lay in a bedroom with another sister, pretending they were angels in heaven, fantasising that they were somewhere else.

The sisters starved Ramos, only feeding him beans on four occasions, and sometimes providing him with a carrot or a piece of cheese. His weight loss was dramatic and he grew painfully weak, weighing only 35 kilograms (78 pounds). He became so ill he vomited anything he ate. He was washed down in the bathroom when his stench became too overpowering for the women.

The man held in the cupboard wasn't entirely a secret. Many family members knew of his situation, as such occurrences of people being locked up in the house were not unique.

Peppi McIntosh, father of Linda Weston's children, visited the apartment while Ramos was held captive. Jean was a toddler at the time and alerted her father to the man's presence. He approached, opened the door and began questioning the man. "He was in there tied up. I told him to get out [of] the closet. I asked him what is he doing there anyway. I say, 'What is you doing in the closet?'"

McIntosh attempted to untie the man, but then asked one of the younger Weston sisters to do it for him.

Ramos' mother reported him missing on November 24, after she noticed she hadn't seen him for about two weeks.

After two months in the closet, Ramos' emaciated body turned purple. Bernardo Ramos died shortly after Christmas, around December 28, 1981.

"Get him out of here," sobbed Linda Weston, when she saw his corpse.

DISPOSAL OF BODY

Family members removed Bernard Ramos' clothes and dressed him in a blue sweatshirt and women's underwear. Alexander and Venus stuffed Ramos's body into a green garbage bag. Using a baby stroller, they wheeled this body through the harsh Philadelphia winter streets, in the early hours of the morning, and dumped him on the floor of an abandoned convent in the 1800 block of Green Street, just a few streets from where Ramos lived.

Two men entered the convent later the same day the

body was dumped and reported their find to authorities. Police noticed the body was stiff, but there was no sign of foul play. The medical examiner ruled that Ramos died of natural causes, succumbing to malnutrition.

On November 12, 1982, police were called to the Weston's home. Linda and Venus had lit a fire inside the apartment, aiming to "set the fire to run the evil spirits out of the closet." They were charged with arson.

TRIAL

On Saturday, January 15, 1983, Linda and Venus Weston were arrested at their new residence in the 1900 block of North 11th Street. They were both charged with murder, kidnapping, and conspiracy. A concerned relative — a teenage girl who lived at the former apartment at the time of the murder — contacted police after a member of the Weston family went missing, suspecting they had been murdered in a similar fashion to Ramos. The girl also feared she would suffer a similar fate because of her knowledge of Ramos' death.

Alexander and Valerie testified against their sisters in a preliminary hearing. On Tuesday, July 12, 1983, Venus Weston pleaded guilty, convicted of third-degree murder. The arson charge was dropped in exchange for her guilty plea. On October 17, 1983, she was sentenced to six to 12 years in prison.

Despite being the mastermind, Linda Weston initially

avoided jail, as she was deemed incompetent to stand trial alongside her sister.

Common Pleas Court Judge John Geisz wrote: "The doctor had performed a psychiatric evaluation on Linda Weston and his report described the defendant as being a mentally retarded young adult suffering from intrinsic brain disease, mainly epilepsy. ... Dr. Grosso also diagnosed the defendant as a schizophrenic."

On December 14, 1984, after being ruled competent, Linda Weston was also found guilty of third-degree murder. She was found not guilty on the charge of arson. Peppi McIntosh testified against her in court. She was sentenced to four to ten years at the maximum-security women's prison, State Correctional Institution, near Muncy, Pennsylvania.

AFTERMATH

On January 15, 1987, Linda Weston was paroled after serving her minimum time, a total of four years, including her two years held at a local prison. She was ordered to undertake intensive supervision and therapy, along with an order that she take psychotropic drugs to stabilise her mental illness. Violating her parole, she returned to prison, but was paroled again on July 8, 1987.

On October 10, 1988, Linda failed to make contact with her parole officer and absconded for five years, avoiding detection of the Pennsylvania Board of Probation and

Parole. She quickly regained custody of her children. By 1993 she eventually fell off the radar and was out of contact with the criminal justice system.

Venus served her minimum term of six years and returned to live in North Philadelphia after her release, where she still resides. Venus claims she has little recall of the events surrounding Barnardo Ramos' death, because of Linda drugging her at the time. She also claims that her sister feigned her mental problems to avoid being properly prosecuted.

Around 1996 Linda assaulted a woman, but when questioned by police she told them Venus had carried out the attack. Venus was arrested and charged. Soon the sister's relationship disintegrated because of the false accusation. Venus also suspected her sister had stolen her identification. Even though the assault charges were later dropped, Venus and Linda never rebuilt their bond.

CHAPTER 03

DAVID BISSON

BRETIGNY-SUR-ORGE, PARIS

– FRANCE.

1982

To the outside world, David Bisson didn't exist, a boy the world almost forgot about entirely. Until his escape there was almost no evidence he had ever been born. When he was discovered after eight years of being locked away, he became known in the French press as "The Cupboard Boy."

LEAD UP TO CRIME

Françoise Bisson was born into a large family. Her mother was a peasant woman, and her father a hopeless alcoholic who left early on. She always had a guarded personality, impenetrable, someone who never quite understood their place in the world and unprepared to let the world in. Her temper saw her fight constantly with her mother, and at age 14 Françoise left home to start a new life in Paris.

While working as a train stewardess on the sleeper cars, she met a singer and soon became pregnant. He would abandon her, leaving her with only six hundred francs and herself to rely on. She didn't stop working while expecting. On May 29, 1970, she hopped off the train in the French town of Angers, went to the hospital and gave birth to David. She left him with a maternity nurse and went back to work.

David spent the first four years of his life in a series of foster homes, where he fondly remembers seaside trips and a kindly old woman. One day his mother came to collect him. She had since settled in with a new man — who David assumed was his father — and had given birth to a second son. David put up a fight as she tried to remove him from foster care. He had no previous memory of her, and felt an instant fearful sense of mistrust.

The reunited family lived in a small third-floor apartment in Neuilly-sur-Marne, France, all sleeping in the same room. During the first year Françoise stayed at home to look after her new baby, and during this time David's beatings began. The beatings would often relate to food, as David had trouble swallowing. He also held a continual silence towards his mother, rarely speaking to her. Françoise's hair-trigger temper saw him punished often, forced to kneel on a metal bar for hours with his nose against the wall. She hit him for no reason, removed his bed, and locked him in a bathroom for days on end.

David told a girl at a child-minder's house about the abuse happening at home. He never saw the child-minder or her daughter again. At four-and-a-half-years-old his mother bound his hands and feet, and locked him in the dark bathroom.

HELD CAPTIVE

David Bisson was chained to a pipe between the sink and the toilet. The shutters were closed, the door locked, and he lost all contact with the outside world. He experienced almost daily beatings at the hands of his mother, mad with a volatile rage, which his stepfather, Claude Bedside, ignored. He was fed leftovers and fruit. On weekends he would be untied as the family went away on holidays, leaving him behind.

His family continued to use the bathroom as usual, while David faced the wall, chained. He remained perfectly still as they went about their daily ablutions. Françoise and Claude even had sex in the bathroom on one occasion, pretending he wasn't there.

David received cold baths and wore little clothing. His half-brother, Laurent, was showered in gifts, took hot bubble baths, and played with toys. Laurent went to school, had friends over to play and celebrated birthdays and Christmases with the family, all while David remained chained to the pipe.

Françoise constantly argued with Claude, but she saved the worst for David. With his hands and feet bound, she lowered him head first into the bath or the flushing toilet. She set his hair on fire, and plunged his hands into boiling water, causing third-degree burns that would leave his fingers webbed. She burnt him with cigarettes, and forced him to eat his own vomit when he couldn't keep his food down. David hid apple seeds behind the toilet, pretending they were cars as he played with them on the side of the bath. When his mother found them she beat him with a stiletto until his skull was exposed.

A fire broke out in the building and it was evacuated. David was left chained inside the apartment as his family fled. Fire fighters put out the flames, but David was not discovered.

On a rare occasion when Claude had friends over, Françoise considered hiding David in the basement, but instead took him for a walk. It was a brief interval. He remembers laughing with her, and seeing cars and planes. That night the beatings resumed.

At age nine he was moved from the bathroom and chained to his parent's bed. He was forced to remain kneeling at the end of their bed, to scared to sleep even while they did. They hid him under the mattress while they had sex above.

David made an escape in August 1980 by scaling down wall from the third floor. As he was climbing out the window he heard a key turn in the front door. He fell and crashed through a garage roof. He was spotted by neighbours and taken to the police. After a month in hospital he was returned home.

The family moved to Bretigny-sur-Orge in July 1981, transporting David in the car under blankets. He was locked in a dark cupboard and forgotten about. He spent up to four days without food at a time. While David was locked in the cupboard he would listen to children playing in the nearby playground. "I often thought of death, but I didn't want to die." He remained hidden there for a year, until one summer day Françoise forgot to lock the apartment door.

ESCAPE

On August 19, 1982, David stepped out of the cupboard, and dressed himself in a jacket and large tennis shoes. He collected loose change, opened the door, and walked outside. He planned to go to his grandma's house, not realising she lived 200 kilometres (125 miles) away.

He wandered the streets, terrified at the sound of every car, thinking it might be his parents. He hid in a garden, curled up under some bushes.

"Is he dead? What's going on?" a group of people wondered.

"Don't send me back home . . ." said David.

After years of silence, David began to tell his story, about the bathroom, the cupboard, and the abuse at the hands of his mother. He was taken to the police station, then to the hospital. It was only because of the work of a young constable that the truth was discovered. David did not exist on public records. Neighbours did not know of his existence, even though they knew of his half-brother who also lived in the house. He was a boy everyone had forgotten about.

David appeared to have the body of a six year old, even though he was now 12. Soon the media arrived and David's story awakened the attention of France. He received public donations of toys.

Laurent was on holiday when David escaped. Both boys were placed in homes by Social Services. His parents were arrested.

TRIAL

David was 15 when his parents went to trial in 1985. When Françoise saw her son, she kissed him. Laurent pleaded with David to write a letter to the judge so the court would show leniency towards their parents. David obliged and their parents received a lighter sentence, but Laurent soon all but forgot he had a brother and abandoned David.

A year after his escape David saw Françoise in prison, she refused to see a psychiatrist, and at trial never admitted to her actions.

Françoise and Claude were jailed for seven years, and broke up while in prison. Françoise was released early towards the end of 1987.

AFTERMATH

David went to school, but remained self-conscious about his disfigured hands. He went through a rebellious phase and expressed bouts of violence. He stayed in homes until he was 20 and gained employment in restaurants.

David was always fond of his grandmother, but during an argument she yelled: "But you're nothing but a bastard." It was the same thing she thought of his mother, her own daughter. He didn't see her after that.

When David felt comfortable he asked his mother about her past — their past. Keeping true to her usual closed-off nature, she moved house without telling anyone, never answering his questions. David learned to forgive her. He married and had two children. He enjoys life's little freedoms. In the past he has occasionally spoken to French media and advocates for other abused children.

The dark brings back memories of his time locked

away, so he sleeps with the light on, and can't stand to be locked away. Françoise Bisson has since died. David Bisson now shuns all media attention and dislikes travelling in public. He is considered disabled because of his experience, but enjoys his life of freedom.

David lives in Paris, a thin figure with deep blue eyes. His memoir is titled L'Enfant Derriere La Porte - *The Boy Behind the Door*.

CHAPTER 04

COLLEEN STAN

RED BLUFF, CALIFORNIA

— UNITED STATES.

1984

On May 19, 1977, Colleen Stan was hitchhiking through the Californian countryside, travelling through the forests of the west coast, to surprise a friend for her birthday. It would be seven years before she would return home. Her prison: a series of small wooden boxes. Her captors: a sadistic husband, and a wife desperate for respite.

LEAD UP TO CRIME

Janice Hooker had allowed her husband to live out his bondage fantasies on her, but when she began to tire, the couple made an agreement to kidnap a female to serve as a replacement for the young mother. There was one condition; Cameron was not to have sex with his new captive.

To the outside world, Cameron Hooker appeared surprisingly normal: a mild mannered small town lumberjack with a bookish demeanour, who lived a relatively quiet life raising his family. Hooker wore soiled work clothes as he drove his cobalt blue Dodge Colt through Red Bluff, California — a town almost forgotten about in the modernisation of America. He spotted Colleen.

Colleen Stan, 20, was used to hitchhiking, a common sight in 1970s America. She attempted to hitchhike from Eugene, Oregon to Westwood, Northern California, almost 640 kilometres (400 miles), to attend a friend's party. In Red Bluff she turned down two offers for a ride. On the third offer she accepted a lift with Cameron Hooker, 23. The ride seemed innocent enough, in the car also travelled his wife, Janice, who held their baby. At a truck stop Colleen went to the bathroom. She sensed something was wrong – a voice in her head told her to run – but she ignored it.

While the kidnapping appeared random, months of

planning had gone into almost every detail. Hooker drove Colleen to a wooded area, where Janice stepped out of the car. Hooker held a knife to Colleen's throat, bound her wrists, ankles and jaw, and affixed a device known as the "head box." The homemade device consisted of two wooden interlocked boxes, padded for soundproofing. Its sole purpose was so no one could hear the victim scream.

They transported her through the mountain roads, before the husband and wife team stopped for an evening meal, leaving Colleen bound in the car.

Colleen was taken to a house at 1140 Oak Street, Red Bluff. Hooker removed the head box, led Colleen inside the house and forced her into the basement.

HELD CAPTIVE

Standing her on an icebox, Hooker strapped Colleen Stan up by her wrists. He pulled the icebox away, leaving her suspended and powerless. Through the pain, Colleen found she could peer out under the blindfold and see the couple having sex in front of her. When Cameron noticed, he whipped her, telling her not to watch. Janice went back upstairs as he continued to torture her. He connected electric clips to her genitals, but the device failed. He set about acting out a series of sadistic sexual fantasies he had witnessed in his collection of BDSM porn.

Colleen was held in a wooden coffin, only let out when Hooker used her as his sex slave, initially keeping her locked inside for four months. When he began releasing her, he forced her to complete household chores. He made her sign a contract: signing away her life to him, becoming his sex slave, and taking the assumed name of K. She was told an overseeing organisation called "The Company" — a slave owners network stretching across the country — monitored every element of her existence and tracked her every action.

On April 28, 1978, the Hooker's moved house, taking Colleen with them. At their new trailer, they kept her in a double-lined box under their marital waterbed. Colleen looked after the couple's two children and was allowed out for jogs, where she would be timed. Her fear of The Company kept her from running away, believing they would come after her and her family.

While Janice was at work, Hooker would rape and torture Colleen.

In 1980 Colleen was taken to a phone box to call her family, but Hooker's finger hovered over the receiver, ready to cut her off if she said anything he didn't like. He later told her The Company had approved a family visit. She was given clear instructions to pretend she was engaged to Cameron, and was told The Company had bugged her parent's house, ready to kill her family if she spoke out. He dropped her off at the house, met her parents, then left.

Her family recognised something was wrong, but were

too afraid to push the issue, fearing Colleen was involved in a cult. They believed if they upset her they would never see her again. Twenty-four hours later, Colleen received a phone call from Hooker, and he collected her from her parent's house. Hooker had achieved a level of "grandiose control," maintaining control over Colleen, even when not present.

Fearing losing this level of power, Hooker returned Colleen to the box under the bed, where she would stay for another three years. His control was now absolute. She was only ever let out when his family were not at home, used as a puppet in his sadistic desires. His children were unaware she was even in the house.

Short on cash, the Hooker's let Colleen out to work in a hotel, in her mind she was still a slave, still afraid of The Company. The sadism against Colleen began to lessen, as Cameron returned his focus back to torturing Janice.

ESCAPE

Janice confessed to a local pastor about what was occurring, who instructed her she was living in sin and that she had to leave the situation. On August 19, 1984, she visited Colleen at the hotel and told her The Company didn't exist.

The next day Colleen called Hooker from a bus station, and said, "I'm getting on a bus. I'm leaving. And there is nothing you can do to stop me." She heard Hooker cry as his world collapsed. Colleen hopped on the bus and finally left Red Bluff.

Colleen travelled to be reunited with her family, following the path she intended to take seven years earlier, but she did not go straight to the police. Instead, she phoned the Hooker's for the next three months, still confused about her relationship to the pair. Meanwhile, Cameron Hooker set to work destroying his beloved torture devices.

Janice finally alerted police, claiming Cameron had also abducted and shot Marie Elizabeth Spannhake in 1976 in what started as a similar abduction to Colleen's. No physical evidence was found to substantiate the claim, though Hooker is still the prime suspect.

When police arrived at the Hooker's trailer, they found an array of torture equipment, along with rolls of photographic evidence depicting Colleen being abused, and the slave contract she had signed.

Police charged Hooker with 17 counts of rape related offences, sodomy and false imprisonment.

TRIAL

At the trial, Colleen sat within feet of Hooker, who smirked during the proceedings.

Physical evidence was brought out and displayed to the court and jury. A reconstructed box — the same Colleen had spent three years in under the bed — housing a mannequin, was positioned in the middle of the courtroom, where it remained throughout the trial.

The defence claimed that even while Colleen had been kidnapped, the actions that followed were all consensual, and she had numerous opportunities to escape but chose to remain. The defence revealed love letters Colleen had written to Hooker, but they were scribed while she was chained to a toilet and crippled by psychological abuse. Colleen had learned to show aspects of love as a survival mechanism, so that Hooker would treat her better. She always signed the letters with her slave name K or Kay.

Janice testified against her husband in exchange for immunity.

The trial lasted five weeks. Found guilty, Cameron Hooker was sentenced to 104 years imprisonment. During sentencing, the judge stated, "I would like to say that I consider this defendant to be the most dangerous psychopath that I have ever dealt with. For no other reason than that he appears to be exactly the opposite of what he is."

As he left the courtroom, Hooker said, "I should have killed her."

AFTERMATH

Colleen Stan managed to put the pieces of her life back together. She still lives in Northern California, and has a close bond with her family. She married but later divorced, and has an adult daughter. She has undergone years of counselling to help her recover and ease her anger towards Hooker. She works with other women who have suffered from abuse.

Colleen wrote a book about her experience, titled *Colleen Stan: The Simple Gifts in Life*.

For her part in the crimes, Janice Hooker was never punished. She works as a social worker and still lives in California. She goes by her maiden name Janice Annette Lashley.

Cameron Hooker will be eligible for parole in 2023. He is housed at Folsom State Prison, California. Appeals in 2010 claiming his rights had been violated were denied.

CHAPTER 05

GARY HEIDNIK

PHILADELPHIA, PENNSYLVANIA

- UNITED STATES.

1987

Gary Heidnik wanted children, but every intimate relationship he had with women disintegrated. He needed to find a way to make sure they would never leave him, so he decided to keep females in his basement. His sadistic desires were the stuff of horror movies, and would become part of the inspiration behind serial killer Buffalo Bill, portrayed in *The Silence of the Lambs*.

LEAD UP TO CRIME

Michael Heidnik pushed his tyrannical nature and racism onto his two boys. He devised punishments for his sons: forcing them to wear bulls-eyes on the seats of their pants so their schoolmates would kick them; hung their sheets out for their neighbours to see after they wet the bed; and hung Gary by his ankles from a third storey window. When he was six, Gary fell out of a tree and suffered brain damage. The injury led him to have a misshapen skull, and the other children called him "football head." It was then that his unusual behaviour began to take hold and he would torture his once loved pets by hanging them.

Gary Heidnik's father disinherited and renounced him in the mid-1960s after he discovered him living with a black woman. He joined the army in his late teens, but was later discharged when he was diagnosed as schizophrenic. He would spend much of his adult life in and out of 21 different mental institutions and he made several suicide attempts.

His alcoholic mother, Ellen Vandervoort, was married five times, twice to African-American men. She committed suicide on Mother's Day 1971 by swallowing mercury as a way of making sure her sons would never forget her. She was found in the basement.

In 1976, Heidnik owned a house in Cedar Avenue, Philadelphia. He had an argument with his girlfriend and shut off the electricity to the building. Another tenant,

Robert Rodgers, climbed through a basement window to find Heidnik sitting on a child's mattress. Heidnik shot at him, grazing his face. Charges were laid, but dropped a week later. When he sold the rubbish filled house, the couple cleaning the premises found a large amount of pornography. They also found a pit where Heidnik had dug through the concrete basement floor.

On May 22, 1978, Heidnik's girlfriend, Anjeanette Davidson, gave birth to their daughter. Anjeanette had an IQ of only 49 and suffered a fibroid tumour, not allowing her to have a natural birth. Their child was placed in foster care after Heidnik barely allowed Davidson to eat during her pregnancy.

While the couple visited Anjeanette's sister, Alberta Davidson, 34, at the Selingrove Centre for the mentally retarded on May 7, 1978, he signed her out with no intention of returning her. Heidnik held Alberta in her sister's basement for ten days, where he repeatedly raped her, tearing her vagina and giving her gonorrhoea. Officials from the centre visited the house with a police escort, after a previous attempt failed to find the missing woman. She was found in a coal bin in the basement. Heidnik was charged with a string of offences, including kidnapping, rape, and false imprisonment. The more serious charges had to be dropped, as Alberta was too mentally handicapped to testify. He was found guilty of interfering with the custody of a committed person, unlawful restraint, and recklessly endangering another person. He was sentenced to three to seven years, and spent just over four years moving through a series of mental institutions. He was released on April 12, 1983, with three years supervision.

Gary Heidnik would impregnate several women, including a mail-order bride from the Philippines. He would not have access to any of his children, with them either placed in foster care or living with their mothers. If he wanted to raise a family of his own, he would have to make sure neither the mothers nor his children could ever leave.

HELD CAPTIVE

Josefina Rivera, 25, was streetwise, running away from a foster home at aged 12 to live on the streets of North Philadelphia, where she would inject cocaine at local flophouses. On November 26, 1986, she had a fight with her boyfriend. She stormed out of the house to prostitute on the corner of Third Street and Girard Avenue, hoping to turn a $20 trick. Gary Heidnik cruised by in his Cadillac Coupe de Ville, the mother of three children hopped inside, and he took her back to his house at 3520 North Marshall Street.

After they completed their deal in an upstairs bedroom, Heidnik choked Rivera, and took her to the dank and dark basement. He fastened a muffler clamp around her ankle and secured the bolt with glue. He left her alone, chained up in the basement.

When Heidnik returned three days later, he brought down his next captive, Sandra Lindsay, 24. She was mentally disabled and went missing while walking to the store. He chained her up in the same fashion as Rivera. He forced the women to watch each other be raped, and used a shovel handle to beat them into submission. Lindsay's mother visited Heidnik's house multiple times over the next few days, searching for her daughter, but there was never an answer at the door.

Lisa Thomas, 19, was a single mother on welfare, who had dropped out of high school to have her baby. As she walked down Lehigh Street on December 22, 1986, Heidnik offered her a lift. She hopped in the car with the stranger. He bought her lunch, where she took an allergy pill. Afterwards, he took her clothes shopping at Sears. Promising her a trip to Atlantic City, he drove her back to his house and gave her a wine. As the wine reacted with the pill, she passed out. He took her upstairs and had sex with her. When she asked to go home, he choked and cuffed her, then pushed her down the stairs into the basement.

Heidnik uncovered a pit — a deep hole burrowing through the concrete that he had spent nine months excavating — where Rivera and Lindsay were confined. He introduced the women, had sex with Thomas again, and then prepared the women sandwiches.

On New Year's Day 1987, Deborah Dudley was brought into the cellar. She made a poor captive for Heidnik — feisty and confrontational. She refused to submit. The cramped and putrid conditions caused Heidnik to do some refining. He bought them a portable toilet, tampons, and allowed them to bathe over consecutive days.

Along with the regular rapes, humiliations, and starvation, Heidnik devised a serious of punishments for any perceived slight he believed the women to be guilty of. He beat them with a shovel handle while stretched on a pool table, forced them into the pit, and suspended them from an eyehook. To prevent them from hearing him move around upstairs, he pushed screwdrivers into their ears to deafen them. Music blared continuously so no one could hear their desperate cries. The already substandard diet was reduced to dog food.

On January 14, while the women were held captive, Heidnik attended court as his Filipino mail-order bride — who fled after only three-and-a-half months marriage and who sent only a postcard alerting him of her pregnancy — sued him for child support. He became evasive when questioned about the finances of the United Church of the Ministers of God, which he ran from his home, estimated to be worth over $550,000. The church provided services to mentally and physically disabled people who didn't feel comfortable attending regular church.

Jacquelyn Askins, 18, had a slight build and was quiet.

She met Heidnik around noon on January 18, 1987, while trying to turn a trick on West Girard Avenue in Poplar. She soon joined the other women in the cellar.

Heidnik thought his plan was unfolding perfectly, believing Rivera and Lindsay were pregnant after they missed their periods, ready to supply him with two of the ten babies he desired. Heidnik was mistaken and the women were not pregnant, which left him disappointed.

Sandra Lindsay was suspended by her wrists from a ceiling beam as punishment for trying to climb out of the pit. A week later, on February 7, she died. Heidnik thought she was faking, so he threw her body back in the pit. He made Rivera, Thomas and himself bowls of ice cream. He retrieved Lindsay's body and carried her upstairs, where he dismembered her with a power saw. He bagged some parts and placed them in the freezer, gave some bones to his dogs, and minced up flesh and mixed it with dog food to feed his captives and pets. Neighbours soon called the police as the sweet-awful smell of roasting flesh crept its way through the city block. Police responded, but soon left after Heidnik told them, "I just burnt my dinner."

Besides providing a meal, Lindsay would also serve as a warning. Dudley refused to comply with Heidnik's authority, so he took her upstairs to show her Lindsay's head boiling away in a pot. When this made little difference to her attitude, Heidnik came up with another plan.

Rivera had been working on Heidnik, attempting to befriend him so she could plot an escape. The favour she garnered from Heidnik had a price. On March 18 he sought to punished Lisa, Jacquelyn, and Deborah, using Josefina to carry out the act. He ordered Josefina to partly fill the pit with water and he lowered the three women into the sludge. He fetched a stripped electrical cord, and made Josefina electrocute the women by touching the bare wires on their chains. On the final jolt, the wires touched the chain around Deborah Dudley's neck, killing her instantly.

Dudley's body was placed in a freezer. A week later Heidnik and Rivera transported the body to New Jersey's Pine Barrens, where they dumped her in the forest. The next day the pair kidnapped Agnes Adams, 24, a prostitute he had already had sex with in the house while the other women were held downstairs. Like all the other victims, she was also African-American. However, with two women dead and none pregnant, Heidnik would have to work harder to see his plan come to fruition.

ESCAPE AND RESCUE

Josefina Rivera convinced Gary Heidnik that if he let her out she would visit a friend and bring her back as the next slave. But, first she needed to visit her family. Heidnik had forced Rivera to write a confession, claiming responsibility for Dudley's death. He believed this protected him from Rivera escaping, as she would incriminate herself.

Parked at a gas station on Sixth and Girard Street, Heidnik left the car running as he waited for Rivera to return. She ran four blocks to the house she shared with her boyfriend, that she had left on a cold November night four months earlier. As Rivera unloaded the details of her ordeal, her boyfriend listened in disbelief. They decided to go back and attack Heidnik, but changed their minds, fearing he might return to North Marshall Street and kill the other women. Instead, they called 911.

Police soon arrived at the gas station and approached the car with their guns drawn.

"Didn't I make my child support?" asked Heidnik.

Police were quick to smash through the front door of Heidnik's house. They found the three women chained up in the basement: Thomas and Askins were asleep on an old mattress; Adams' was found handcuffed in the pit and police lifted her out of the hole. In the kitchen, human remains were found in a roasting pan and a forearm discovered in the freezer.

"Gary kept ice cream in the freezer. Can we eat that?" asked Agnes Adams, as police escorted the women from the house.

TRIAL

On March 25, 1987, Heidnik's nose was broken when attacked by a fellow prisoner. A week later, on April 2, he attempted suicide by trying to hang himself in the shower with a t-shirt.

Heidnik was charged with a slew of offences, including: murder, possession and abuse of a corpse, kidnapping, rape, making terroristic threats, indecent assault, and involuntary deviate sexual intercourse.

Throughout the trial, the testimony indicated the other captives felt Rivera received preferential treatment from Heidnik, which caused jealousy amongst the women, though she would be ultimately responsible for their rescue.

On July 1, 1988, Gary Heidnik was found guilty on two counts of first-degree murder and sentenced to death on each count. He appeared unmoved as the verdict was read, tranquilised by 300 milligrams of thorazine. Other charges he was found guilty of were: kidnapping - six counts; rape - five counts; aggravated assault - four counts; and involuntary deviate sexual intercourse - one count.

Heidnik was housed at the State Correctional Institute in Pittsburgh, where he waited to be executed by electric chair. On January 3, 1989, he left prison and was admitted to the State Penn Hospital in a semi-comatose state, after he attempted suicide by overdosing on thorazine.

"The ironic thing is now they're going to work on him around the clock so he can regain consciousness so we can execute him," said Heidnik's attorney.

After a number of delays, Gary Heidnik was executed by lethal injection on July 6, 1999, at Rockview State

Penitentiary in Benner, Pennsylvania. A final appeal was made to save his life, claiming Heidnik was mentally incompetent, but it delayed his death by only 45 minutes. He was pronounced dead at 10:29 p.m. Even anti-death penalty activists were notably absent from his execution. No one claimed his body and he was cremated.

AFTERMATH

Heidnik's estate was divided amongst his victims and the families of the deceased.

The women made attempts to re-adjust to normal life. Most have remained out of the public eye, though attention was never far away in the suburbs of North Philadelphia. They were known as the "Heidnik girls," and people regularly called out "Alpo" after the brand of dog food they were fed.

After the trial, Josefina Rivera lost custody of her children, and fell back into drugs and prostitution, rather than seeking therapy. She remains tormented by Heidnik and still sees reminders of him everywhere: in food packaging, in men with beards, and in holes in the ground. She has appeared in print interviews on the anniversaries of their liberation. She was reunited with her children on Christmas 2010. She was last known to live in New Jersey.

Jacquelyn Askins appeared on *The Steve Wilkos Show* episode "I Survived a Serial Killer," where she explained her story in detail. She described how the captivity made her unsure of what she would become once she was released, fearing she would turn into a person similar to Heidnik. She spent five years in and out of mental institutions to recover from post-traumatic stress disorder, and still bears the mental and physical scars of her ordeal.

The house at 3520 North Marshall Street has been sold since Heidnik lived there, though the sale price has always remained painfully low. In 2003 the house sat in a state of disrepair, abandoned, and unfit for human habitation. Trash was strewn around the block and filled the basement where the horrors took place. The appearance of the house was altered drastically in an attempt to distance it from its past. As of 2012 it appeared to be somewhat occupied.

CHAPTER 06

KATIE BEERS

BAY SHORE, LONG ISLAND, NEW YORK

– UNITED STATES

1992

Katie Beers' life was one of constant struggle from the moment she was born. Surrounded by abject poverty, a dysfunctional family, and sexual predators, Katie became streetwise at a very young age, running errands for her family at all hours of the night through the streets of New York. While the adults around her ignored her needs, John Esposito was making plans for the nine-year-old.

LEAD UP TO CRIME

In 1977, John Esposito attempted to abduct a seven-year-old boy from a shopping mall. He was caught and pleaded guilty to attempted aggravated harassment and placed on probation. Though he would lay low for many years, what desires drove him would eventually resurface in much more sinister ways. Rejected from joining mentoring programs for children of single-parent homes in 1980, Esposito used supermarket bulletin boards in an attempt to secure his prey.

Long before Katie Beers was abducted and held captive, she was already a child in a dangerous and perilous situation. She was a girl neglected and let down by the adults in her life. She had a long history with Social Services and was known in the neighbourhood as "the cockroach kid." She was also known in the area of West Islip, Long Island, as a girl who lacked parental guidance, roaming the streets, running errands for family members, and barefoot and poorly dressed in the dead of winter. She lived with her single mother and other adults who formed a makeshift family, residing in a dilapidated house that from the outside resembled a car-wrecking yard, in a neighbourhood struck with chronic poverty.

Marilyn Beers, 43, was never sure who Katie's father was, having fallen pregnant during a night of bar hopping, she gave up her child to Linda Inghilleri, 39, who became Katie's godmother and surrogate parent. Linda was married to Salvatore (Sal) Inghilleri, 39, who was physically and sexually abusing Katie. He also killed her cat by throwing it against a wall.

The nine-year-old missed a lot of school. Instead, she stayed home to complete chores, go shopping for cigarettes, and wash clothes at the laundromat.

John Esposito was a friend of the Beers family, and Marilyn trusted him with Katie, believing he was gay. In 1991 Marilyn Beers reported Esposito to police for molesting her 16-year-old son, John Beers, known as "Little John," with the abuse beginning when he was seven. Esposito "Big John" would lavish Little John with gifts, and invited him and his friends to his house that was stocked with videogames and toys.

When sitting in Esposito's truck, Little John was told, "I'm looking for another kid. You're getting too old." That's when Big Johns attention turned towards John Beers' sister Katie.

HELD CAPTIVE

On December 28, 1992, Katie disappeared from the Spaceplex indoor amusement park on Long Island. She was visiting with Esposito, now a 43-year-old contractor, who was treating her to a day out for her tenth birthday, which was two days away.

"I've been kidnapped by a man with a knife," Katie's terrified voice screamed on her godmother's answering machine. "Oh my God. He's coming back."

Hundreds of police searched across Long Island, but there was one place they were focusing on specifically.

John Esposito lived at 1416 Saxon Avenue, Bay Shore, New York. At the property he had constructed a playground, basketball court, swimming pool, and deck. But, 18-months earlier, beneath the converted garage, which he used as an office, he had constructed an underground dungeon. Katie would play in the mound of dirt as Esposito excavated the site.

To enter the bunker, a bookshelf had to be moved, the floor coverings lifted, and a 90 kilogram (200 pound) concrete slab had to be hoisted by an electric wrench, to reveal a vertical shaft that dropped three metres (10 feet) to a soundproof chamber. Preparing for a lengthy stay, Esposito fitted the dungeon with a porcelain toilet lined with black plastic, dehumidifiers, heating, ventilation, television monitors, and a separate containment cell for his captive to sleep in.

Chained around the neck, Katie was held captive for 16 days in the small bunk-box, with only the television to keep her company and to light the darkness. She noticed what looked like blood on the sheets and wondered if others had been held there before her.

Esposito visited her daily to bring fast food and sexually abuse her. One night they watched and episode of *America's Most Wanted* together, where Katie's abduction was featured. Her captor left a voice-activated tape-recorder in the enclosure so he could listen back as she called for help. One recording contained Katie singing "Happy Birthday" to herself on the day she turned ten.

Esposito appeared on television news reports, distraught and pleading for Katie's safe return, but police were already focusing their attention on Esposito, tracking him 24-hours a day, following him through supermarkets and pressuring his family.

RESCUE

Police interviewed Esposito, but released him after 18-hours of questioning. They noticed unaccounted periods of time, and also began wondering if he was a paedophile. Police had searched Esposito's property three times, initially finding Katie's coat and hat in the back of his pick-up truck. Inside his house they found her purse. While Katie was trapped underground she watch police search the premises via close-circuit television, screaming for help.

On January 13, 1993, the pressure got to Esposito and he led police to the dungeon where he held Katie captive. Police unbolted the bookcase, made their way through the two tunnels and three doors, where they heard Katie's small voice say, "I'm here."

Katie was delivered to the back of a waiting police vehicle in front of news crews. She told police how

Esposito had forced her to make a tape recording that he would later play to Linda Inghilleri's answering machine. Esposito had also told Katie that he expected to keep her held captive for over a year.

Esposito justified his actions by claiming he abducted Katie to save her from her troubled family life.

TRIAL

Katie testified against John Esposito before a grand jury. Esposito made a plea bargain, pleading guilty to first-degree kidnapping. He admitted he constructed the dungeon for the sole purpose of holding Katie captive. On July 21, 1994, John Esposito was sentenced to 15 years to life in prison. Bowing his head before the court, sobbing, he apologised to Katie and asked for her forgiveness.

Katie also testified against Salvatore Inghilleri, who was charged with sexual abuse and endangering the welfare of a child. Wearing a pink dress, Katie took the stand. Sitting on a pillow — smiling out to school friends when she entered — Katie testified for almost four hours. She had previously been afraid to speak out about the abuse because of Inghilleri's violent nature, as he would strike her across her face leaving marks that would last a week and punch her. He also picked her up by the shirt and abused her animals.

Sal Inghilleri was found guilty and sentenced to four to twelve years imprisonment in August 1994.

AFTERMATH

Marilyn Beers never regained custody of Katie, nor did Linda Inghilleri, as she wasn't a blood relative. John Beers was charged with house burglary in September 1994. Marilyn Beers was charged with social security fraud at the same time.

A family in East Hampton, New York, fostered Katie, raising her with their own four children. They provided structure, discipline, and safety. Katie and her new family sought a life away from the media attention and refused further interviews. She returned to school, which she enjoyed, and was reported to be doing well. She later graduated high school with honours.

Katie graduated from business management at college after attending on a scholarship. She lives in central Pennsylvania, sells insurance, and is married with two children. In January 2013 she released her memoir *Buried Memories*. While she has left much of her past behind, she still occasionally talks to her mother, and recognises the events relating to her kidnapping saved her from the cycle of abuse and presented her with better life opportunities.

Sal Inghilleri was paroled in 2006 and released from prison. He was arrested again in October 2007 for breaking Megan's Law – failing to inform authorities of a change of address. He died of a heart attack in prison in February 2009.

John Esposito is still held at Sing Sing Correctional

Facility in New York. He was denied parole in 2007, 2009 and 2011. He still believes that he is someone whose intention it is to save children from troubled home lives. The parole board considers him a danger to society. He will face the parole board again in September 2013.

CHAPTER 07

MARC DUTROUX

CHARLEROI, HAINAUT – BELGIUM.

1996

Marc Dutroux became known as "The Monster of Belgium," a psychopath who preyed on young females. His arrest would shock Belgium society, resulting in the largest protest the country had ever witnessed, almost overthrowing the Government. Failures by the justice system allowed Dutroux to leave behind a trail of bodies and shattered lives.

LEAD UP TO CRIME

Marc Dutroux grew up with a domineering mother and abusive father, experiencing a loveless childhood with many violent beatings. His parents were both school teachers who displayed egotistical traits, which were passed on to their son. After their separation in 1971, Marc Dutroux left home at 15 and grew into a petty criminal and a teenage prostitute, surviving by servicing older men. Dutroux established a long criminal history: involving stolen luxury cars, muggings, and drug dealing. The unemployed electrician amassed seven houses through the proceeds of crime and benefit fraud.

In 1986 Dutroux and Michelle Martin, school teacher, were convicted for the abduction and rape of five girls. In 1989 Dutroux was sentenced to 13 years for his crimes. Martin received a sentence of five years.

Michelle Martin was Dutroux's mistress, their affair causing the breakup of his marriage from his first wife, which separated him from his two children. Dutroux married Martin in a prison ceremony in 1989, and they went on to have three children together. Belgium police described Michelle Martin as a masochistic woman, who never turned away from her husband's crimes.

Dutroux was released in 1992, after serving only three years. During his parole Dutroux continued to commit further offences. His houses were left mostly unoccupied, and he constructed two dungeons at different locations so he could resume his sadistic crime spree. The parole board would receive a letter, penned by Dutroux's mother, warning authorities that she believed her son was holding young girls captive in the basement of one of his houses. The letter was ignored.

HELD CAPTIVE

Mélissa Russo and Julie Lejeune

On June 24, 1995, two eight-year-old girls, Mélissa Russo and Julie Lejeune, were kidnapped in Grâce-Hollogne, 90 kilometres (56 miles) northeast of Charleroi, Belgium. The pair was held in the house owned by Dutroux and Martin, at Route de Philippeville 128, in the Charleroi suburb of Marcinelle. The girls were repeatedly raped and tortured, their abuse recorded on video.

Dutroux was arrested on December 6, 1995, for organised criminal activity related to stealing luxury cars. He spent three months in prison, leaving Mélissa and Julie in the prison he had constructed. As they waited helplessly in the cage, hidden in the basement, the girls drew pictures on the walls.

Michelle Martin was placed in charge of looking after the children. While she would feed their pet German Shepherds, she neglected to feed Mélissa and Julie, claiming she was too scared, fearing the girls would attack her.

On December 13, 1995, police searched Dutroux's house during the car theft investigation. A locksmith heard the cries of the girls, but was dismissed by the officer in charge, saying it was children playing in the street. Videos of Dutroux building his dungeon were found, but the tapes were never watched, as the police claimed they didn't have a video player.

Both girls starved to death.

Dutroux was released from prison on March 20, 1996. The girls' bodies were placed in garbage bags and buried in the backyard of a house in Sars-la-Buissière. The body of Bernard Weinstein, a former accomplice of Dutroux, was also found buried at the same site.

An Marchal and Eefje Lambrecks

On August 22, 1995, An Marchal, 17, and Eefje Lambrecks, 19, were holidaying with friends in Blankenberge on the Belgium coast, 163 kilometres (100 miles) northwest of Charleroi. For An it was her first time away without her parents and a step towards adult independence. The pair went missing after participating in a hypnotist show at Casino Blankenberge, kidnapped by Dutroux and his accomplice Michel Lelièvre.

Police set up a camera in a train car across from Dutroux's Marcinelle house, as part of Operation Othello to monitor Dutroux, suspecting him of related crimes. But police only activated the camera during business hours, between 8 a.m. and 6 p.m., shutting off the camera at night. The police missed recording Dutroux and Lelièvre move the girls into the house.

As Mélissa Russo and Julie Lejeune were still alive at the time and already being held in the basement, the teenagers were chained to a bed in an upstairs room. Reports of the girls' disappearances were made by their parents, but were ignored by police.

Around two months later, An Marchal and Eefje Lambrecks were drugged with Rohypnol, and they were bound, gagged with tape, and repeatedly raped. They were buried alive under a shed floor at Rue Daubresse 63, Jumet.

Sabine Dardenne

On May 28, 1996, Sabine Dardenne, 12, was riding to school when she was pulled into a van and kidnapped by Dutroux. His accomplice, homeless heroin addict, Michel Lelièvre, assisted him.

Sabine was driven to the house in the decaying industrial heartland of Charleroi, and carried inside in a metal trunk. She was drugged, had a collar fixed around her neck, and was chained to a bed in an upstairs room. Dutroux told Sabine her parents had refused to pay her ransom, and it was his duty to kill her. Instead, he claimed, he was now protecting her and keeping her alive. In return for his protection, he told Sabine, she must provide him with favours. He repeatedly raped her.

After three days Sabine was unchained and moved to a purpose built basement dungeon, imprisoned where the previous two captives, Mélissa Russo and Julie Lejeune, had died.

Sabine kept a journal of the abuse, and wrote thirty letters to her family that Dutroux promised to send, but never did; it was part of the immense psychological torture. If Sabine disobeyed Dutroux demands, he threatened he would hand her over to a gang to be tortured and killed. He also told Sabine that her parents had abandoned their search for her.

Terrorised, drugged, and lonely, Sabine asked if she could have a friend. Dutroux was only too happy to oblige.

Laetitia Delhez

On August 9, 1996, Laetitia Delhez, 14, was abducted after leaving a swimming pool. She was dragged into a white van. A local resident recorded details of the van and the number plate. It belonged to Marc Dutroux.

Sabine had been held for 72 days, and when Dutroux delivered Laetitia, he said to her, "Look what I've done for you."

Laetitia was imprisoned in the basement with Sabine, where Dutroux would abuse both girls while he filmed the assaults.

She would be held for six days.

RESCUE

On August 13, 1996, Dutroux, Martin and Lelièvre were arrested because of the investigation into Delhez's abduction. Lelièvre and Martin confessed to the kidnapping of Laetitia. Dutroux would also confess to the abduction of Sabine. Police found Sabine and Laetitia hidden in the putrid basement dungeon. The girls were weak, starved, and wore only thin summer tops and shorts. The distraught girls were led from the house to an awaiting police car, unshielded from the hungry media, who broadcast the scene across the globe.

The media were also waiting as the girls were reunited with their families on the doorsteps of their homes.

TRIAL

During the assessment of Dutroux, he wasn't labelled fundamentally as a paedophile, but rather a psychopath and serial killer.

Within Belgium unrest was growing as people suspected a police cover-up, wondering if Dutroux had connections to high-ranking officials. Dutroux made claims he was part of a complex paedophile network, integrated into the highest levels of Belgium society, for which he would supply underage girls.

Investigative Judge Jean-Marc Connerotte, who headed the case, was sacked for attending a fundraising dinner with the families of the victims; such a dinner was not an uncommon practice in Belgium. This led to public outrage, believing a massive cover-up was underway, as high-ranking Government officials attempted to hide their own involvement in an expansive paedophile network.

Frustrated at the inadequacies of the Belgium justice system to handle the Dutroux case, citizens descended upon the capital, to form the largest protest the country had ever witnessed. Known as "The White March," 300,000 citizens descended on Brussels on October 20, 1996, their faith in the justice system torn. Calls were made for police to take crimes against children more seriously. Workers went on strike, and firemen hosed down government buildings to symbolise the washing away of corruption. The protests almost pushed Belgium to the cusp of civil revolution. Claims were made that 20 people who had information about the paedophile network, or were connected to the case, allegedly died in suspicious circumstances before the case made it to court.

On April 23, 1998, Dutroux escaped from custody as he was transported to court. He stole a gun from a sleeping guard's belt, and overpowered his way to escape. He stole a car and fled into the country, with 5,000 police officers searching for him. Three hours later he was captured after his car became bogged in a forest, and was spotted by a solitary forest ranger.

It would be eight years until the trial of Marc Dutroux, Michelle Martin, and Michel Lelièvre was underway.

Sabine Dardenne was now 20 years old. Sabine testified that Dutroux was her only abuser and she didn't witness anything to indicate a paedophile ring. Dutroux never gave any information that would expose the network he claimed existed. While the claims were eventually disproven, they caused significant delays to his trial as they were investigated.

On June 17, 2004, Dutroux was found guilty of kidnapping, rape and the murder of four people; he was sentenced to life imprisonment. Dutroux is currently held at Prison de Nivelles, Belgium.

Michelle Martin was found guilty of conspiracy to kidnap and rape. She was sentenced to 30 years in prison and is held at Berkendael-Berkendaal in Brussels.

Michel Lelièvre was found guilty of kidnapping and drug dealing, and sentenced to 25 years in prison.

AFTERMATH

Sabine Dardenne detailed her ordeal in her book *I Choose to Live*; written in the hope she could finally be left alone, free from questioning, and ultimately forgotten about. She does not ask for sympathy, and finds it almost as hard to deal with as the captivity. She rejected much aftercare, including the services of psychiatrists. She believes she would have been sent mad by their questioning and analysing. Her strong will has refused her allow to conform to the role of victim, and she considers the ordeal over with. She considers Dutroux a sick man: who at 12 years old she was unfortunate enough to meet, someone who was never capable of telling the truth, and someone she considers pathetic.

On August 28, 2012, Michelle Martin was released from prison and transferred to a convent, where she will spend at least another ten years of her sentence. Her early release from prison caused further outrage throughout Belgium. She had served only 16 years of her 30-year sentence.

Around November 25, 2012, the process for Marc Dutroux's parole was set in motion. He was eligible for parole after serving 17 years of his life sentence. The parole request is a requirement of Belgium law, through the Court of Execution of Punishment in Brussels. On February 18, 2013, he was denied early release after being found unsuitable for home confinement with electronic monitoring.

CHAPTER o8

ALEXANDER KOMIN

VYATSKIYE POLYANY, KIROV OBLAST

— RUSSIA.

1997

Alexander Komin sought out people who would not be
missed: alcoholic, homeless, and forgotten. He lured them
with the promises of work, shelter, and drink. Deep under
the hard, icy ground of the former Soviet Union, Komin
was building a colony of slaves.

LEAD UP TO CRIME

Vyatskiye Polyany is located in Kirov Oblast, Russia, almost 1,000 kilometres (600 miles) east of Moscow. The industrial town is situated along the banks of the Vyatka River, and in 1997 it supported nearly 45,000 inhabitants. The town's economy revolved around the Molot factory, which produced military machinery.

In 1971, when Alexander Komin (Александр Комин) was on the verge of adulthood, and about to enter into the army, he was convicted for hooliganism after being involved in a street fight and sentenced to three years in prison. During his sentence, Komin worked in a garment factory colony, a job he enjoyed. He met a fellow prisoner named Bigley, who was convicted for holding homeless people in his basement, forcing them to make wooden toys.

On release, Komin became a qualified tailor, but he found work difficult to come by in Vyatskiye Polyany after many of the garment factories closed. Instead, he gained employment as a labourer, security guard, and electrician.

The collapse of the Soviet Union in 1991 saw abject poverty sweep the country, but many people were able to gain property rights. Some of those people were allowed to own garages. Komin took ownership of garage number 198, tucked away amongst a series of dilapidated garages lining a dirt track, resembling a row of modern day storage sheds. A small wicket gate, cut into the main rusted cream painted door, allowed access to the garage.

Komin drew the assistance of accomplice Alexander Mikheyev, a local security guard and friend. For four years they dug the shaft and excavated the rooms. A trapdoor was cut into the wooden floor of the cramped garage, and a 12 metre (40 foot) shaft was dug, squared off, and lined with bricks. Three doors sealed the bunker, one a large metal door stolen from a military base. A metal ladder clung to one wall of the shaft, allowing access to the underground chambers.

Komin's plans were ambitious and entrepreneurial. His goal was to build an underground factory and fill it with female slaves, who would work for his profit and submit for his pleasure. His plans were even greater, with his ultimate aim of establishing an underground city completely colonised by slaves.

The two room subterranean factory was fitted with sewing machines and overlockers. A three-bunk bedroom was built for his slaves, along with a toilet and kitchen. He provided bedding and a television, and lined the walls with wallpaper and pornographic photographs. Electrical wire webbed its way across the brick walls and through the tunnels and rooms.

"Of course, such a crazy idea would not come to a normal man," Komin said. "But still, I think I am normal."

With his factory complete, all Alexander Komin needed was the slaves to populate it, so he could begin production.

HELD CAPTIVE

Alexander Komin had an eye on his neighbour, Vera Tolpayeva, 33, who appeared to be a perfect victim. On January 13, 1995, Komin engaged Tolpayeva in a round of heavy drinking for the Old New Year holiday, celebrated by members of the Russian Orthodox Church. She was invited to the garage, where her vodka was laced with the sedative clonidine. After she woke in the bunker, Komin would soon discover Tolpayeva was not a suitable slave, as she had no desire to learn how to sew.

Komin used Vera Tolpayeva to secure more captives, with each successful mission gaining her more favours and freedoms. She contacted her tailor friend, Tatyana Melnikova, and gave her details on the location of the garage so they could meet. Losing her way, Komin went out to find Melnikova. He met Nikolai Malykh, also a tailor, who happened to be Tatyana Melnikova's boyfriend. The pair was invited back to the garage where they drank with Komin, only to wake in the bunker.

Nikolai Malykh had served time for robbery, and ranked higher in the criminal hierarchy than Komin. Threatened by the presence of a stronger male, Komin drugged Nikolai Malykh, and with Alexander Mikheyev's help, dumped him in a snow-covered field in the countryside, where he would become lost under the drifts. His body would be found a week later, but police suspected he drank too much moonshine vodka, wandered off, and froze to death.

Tatyana Melnikova was forced to make gowns, boxer shorts and pants, which Komin sold at local markets. As his business grew, Komin decided he needed more physical labour to expand his bunker.

On March 21, 1995, he used his traditional methods of offering employment and alcohol to take alcoholic Yevgeny Shishov captive, with Komin believing Shishov would be easy to control and could dig extra rooms in the underground prison. Komin had made a mistake.

There was no chance of the slaves reaching the metal door and attempting to escape; 220 volts electrified the ladder leading up the shaft to the exit. However, Shishov was a qualified electrician and former paratrooper. He could easily disable the homemade security system. He was strapped to a chair and bound in electrical wires. The two female captives were given a switch each and told to flick them. Tatyana Melnikova refused, but Vera Tolpayeva was threatened; soon to suffer the same fate if she did not comply because of her expendable position and her refusal to complete manual labour. She pressed a switch and sent a jolt of electricity, killing Shishov. His body was removed with the aid of a winch and dumped in a field.

Komin and Vera Tolpayeva set out to find a new slave.

Tatyana Kozikova had worked as a cook in Ulyanovsk. She had spent two years in prison, and on July 21, 1995, she was to appear at the District Court of Vyatskiye

Polyany. She did not attend court and had not been seen for a week. Instead she had met Komin and Tolpayeva at a train station, who offered her alcohol and employment. She was drugged and set to work in the factory.

The victims were shackled to walls and chained around the ankle while they worked 16 hour shifts. They were beaten with a rubber hose, and raped on Komin's whim. As punishment they were made to rub themselves with their own excrement. The captives made dance costumes, gowns, and robes for priests. They also created highly detailed religious tapestries and vestments for the church.

The two Tatyana's made a plan. They locked Komin in a room, but before they could escape, he broke free. After this attack, Komin enforced new security measures. He rigged up a red light to flash, signalling he was about to descend into the bunker. The prisoners locked themselves into a wire collar and waited for Komin to enact his torture. As retribution for the escape attempt, Komin and Mikheyev tattooed the women's faces, carving the word "раб" (slave) on their foreheads. The women chose tattooing over the other option of having their mouths sliced from ear to ear — a form of torture known as a "Glasgow smile."

While scouting for a new slave Vera Tolpayeva went missing. Komin was concerned she would go to the police but they never arrived. He took to scouting on his own.

Tatyana Nazimova was ill, suffering from leukaemia

and mental illness. Komin approached her at a train station. He now had three slave women, all with the name Tatyana. Tatyana Nazimova would prove to be an unsuccessful slave. She was too ill to work, had no work ethic, but she was attractive. She was taken as a sex slave, used predominantly by Mikheyev. After a year, he grew tired of her, and illness was wasting her body. Komin forced her to drink brake fluid, from which she took days to die.

Komin offered to feed his captives Tatyana Nazimova's body. Instead, he decided to dump Nazimova on the doorstep of the local morgue as a twisted joke. He placed her body on a sled, but was almost caught by a passer-by. Her emaciated corpse was found in a field near the garage. Police believe she suffered a similar fate as the others, and her death was the result of drinking moonshine vodka.

Alexander Komin found Vera Tolpayeva again, at a train station sometime in January 1997. He offered her money if she returned to work for him, finding new markets to sell his garments and sourcing new slaves. She reappeared at the garage a few days later with 23 year-old, blonde haired, Irina Ganushina.

Tolpayeva would soon suffer a similar fate as Nikolai Malykh and Tatyana Nazimova, after she demanded weekly payments from Komin. But, it was Komin who gave her an ultimatum; she decided to drink antifreeze rather than have it forcibly injected into her veins. Her death would take only a few hours, dying with both Tatyana's watching on.

The new captive surprised Komin, and he fell in love with Irina Ganushina. He proposed and bought her a wedding dress. She complied with his wishes after he made threats against her two-year-old child.

RESCUE

On July 21, 1997, in the heat of summer, Irina Ganushina was taken back to Komin's apartment. She was allowed out so they could plan their wedding, but when she was left briefly unattended she made her escape. She ran to the local police station to report the horrific crimes, but police were sceptical of her claims. When she listed the names of her fellow captives the police demanded the location of the underground factory.

Komin was arrested near his garage. Even while apprehended he enacted a final plan and directed a rescuing police officer down the electrified staircase. The officer didn't take the bait.

The two Tatyana's were removed from the underground chamber. Their eyes were covered by black armbands, as authorities were worried the women would be blinded by the harsh daylight that they had not witnessed in over two years. Tatyana Melnikova, 37, and Tatyana Kozikova, 38, had survived, but their faces were tattooed and they had aged dramatically, far beyond their years.

TRIAL

Komin was initially silent upon his arrest, but soon made full confessions and escorted police officials to the scenes of his crimes. The Kirov regional court convicted Alexander Komin on four counts of murder, three counts of illegal detention, illegal entrepreneurship, and use of slave labour.

On June 11, 1999, Alexander Komin was sentenced to life in prison.

Alexander Mikheyev was convicted for the same crimes as Komin and sentenced to 20 years in prison.

AFTERMATH

On June 15, 1999, Alexander Komin committed suicide in prison, four days after learning of his sentence. He severed his femoral artery, while detained in a holding cell, and bled to death. Komin was buried in the same cemetery as his victims, much to the horror of their relatives.

Tatyana Melnikova and Tatyana Kozikova sought compensation through a civil suit, for the moral damage caused to them under Komin's reign. The court decided to grant them ownership of the garage, and the underground prison, as compensation.

Tatyana Melnikova and Tatyana Kozikova moved in with each other after their release, sharing a one-room apartment owned by Melnikova's mother. Both women lived in desperate poverty, with Melnikova scavenging through garbage to find food, because she could not secure her identification papers to obtain welfare.

A public donation fund was established to raise US$400 to remove their facial tattoos. In the demoralised new Russia, not one rouble was donated to remove the markings of their captivity. Tatyana Melnikova died in poverty, still wearing Komin's branding.

In 2009, the Molot factory became unprofitable, and closed in 2010. Its closure saw workers unpaid for months, causing more residents to flee the declining town of Vyatskiye Polyany.

The gruesome events played out by Alexander Komin featured in a documentary series called *Criminal Russia*, screened on Russian television. The episode featuring Alexander Komin was watched by millions, including Victor Mokhov, who rather than become horrified by what he saw, he would instead become inspired.

CHAPTER 09

FUSAKO SANO

KASHIWAZAKI, NIIGATA PREFECTURE

- JAPAN.

2000

Almost a decade after going missing, Fusako Sano approached police officers who had been called to a hospital. She identified herself and explained she had not stepped outside since Nobuyuki Satō kidnapped her in 1990. The case would become known throughout Japan as "The Niigata Girl Confinement Incident."

LEAD UP TO CRIME

In 1990, nine-year-old schoolgirl Fusako Sano was attending school in Sanjo, Japan. Sanjo is located 250 kilometres (155 miles) northwest of Tokyo, and originally formed from a collection of villages. At the time it had a population of around 85,000. It has a river port, a long history of producing metal tools, and is prone to flooding in torrential rains. The Sano family owned rice paddies that they worked.

Nobuyuki Satō lived in the seaside city of Kashiwazaki on Japan's northwestern seaboard, southwest of Sanjo. Satō was an unemployed, 28-year-old male, who lived with his mother, occupying the upstairs floor of her house. Satō's father died in 1989, and afterwards his neighbours noticed that his behaviour became increasingly erratic. His violent outbursts resulted in him breaking the windows and doors of his mother's home. His aggression also turned towards his mother, who neighbours claimed once had a black eye. In the same year, Satō came to the attention of police after he attempted to kidnap a young girl. He was unsuccessful and while on probation he made his second attempt.

On November 13, 1990, Fusako Sano was in the fourth grade, when she watched an afternoon game of baseball at her school with two friends. After the game finished she walked home alone.

Satō drove the 57 kilometre (35 mile) journey from

Kashiwazaki to neighbouring Sanjo, where he kidnapped Fusako Sano at knifepoint, forcing her into the trunk of his car, before returning home. A large police search was soon underway, but police were unable to find the missing schoolgirl.

HELD CAPTIVE

Satō took Fusako from his car and moved her upstairs, where he held her captive in his bedroom for almost a decade. Satō had banned his mother from his bedroom during his teens, restricting her to the downstairs storey of the house. Satō suffered from mental illness and kidnapped Fusako because he desperately wanted someone to talk to and keep him company.

Fusako was bound for several months and had adhesive tape placed over her mouth. Satō ordered her to videotape horse races on the television, and if she made a mistake he would punish her by using a stun gun. Other punishments included being punched and threatened with a knife.

Satō cut Fusako's hair short and made her wear his clothes. Fusako spent most of her time listening to the radio, and during the final year of captivity she was allowed to watch television. Satō provided her with three meals a day, cooked by his mother, or instant food. The door had no lock, but Fusako was banned from touching it. If she attempted to flee, Satō threatened to abandon her alone in the mountains.

If Satō's mother attempted to venture upstairs he would turn violent. His violence escalated and his behaviour became more erratic, causing his mother to make a series of calls to the social workers at the Niigata Health Centre. When workers attended the house they found the girl and ask the police for help. The police refused to assist and told the social workers to sort out the problem themselves.

As Satō's unpredictable behaviour increased, he went with Fusako to the hospital. When he started acting violently towards staff, the police were called. A thin, jaundice girl, barely able to walk, approached police and told them her name was Fusako Sano and that she had been abducted.

"For nine years, I did not take a step out of the house. Today I went outside for the first time," Fusako told police.

When high-ranking police officials were notified of the discovery of the missing girl they had little interest in the matter, deciding instead to play mah-jong.

RESCUE

Fusako was rescued on January 28, 2000. She was now 19 years old, and had been held captive for a total of nine years, two months and 15 days. She was weak and dehydrated. She also suffered serious injuries, including: atrophied leg muscles, where legs are weakened through lack of use; sustained learning difficulties; and would go on to develop post-traumatic stress disorder. Because of her lack of socialisation, and despite her age, she still behaved like a child.

Nobuyuki Satō's mother, now 73, claimed she was unaware that Fusako was living upstairs.

"I was too scared to escape and eventually lost the energy to escape," Fusako reported to police.

Fusako Sano was reunited with her parents who had always remained hopeful of seeing their daughter again.

The news quickly sent shockwaves across Japan, dominating the media. The police were called incompetent, and questions were asked as to why police in neighbouring cities had not worked together on the case. Japan also questioned its sense of community and why neighbours had not noticed anything.

Satō was now 37. He was taken for psychiatric evaluation on January 28, 2000, and formally arrested on February 11 once discharged from hospital. He was diagnosed with several personality disorders, but was still competent to be responsible for his actions, so he was deemed fit to undergo questioning.

Police would claim they had discovered Fusako, but would later have to admit they lied and initially refused to help social workers. The public response to the case would question why the police had not investigated Satō earlier based on his earlier abduction attempt, as he was on probation for a similar crime. Shortly after, several high-ranking police officials resigned, including the Niigata

Prefectural Police Chief Koji Kobayashi.

TRIAL

Nobuyuki Satō pleaded guilty before the Niigata District Court in May 2000 to abducting a minor and unlawful confinement resulting in injury.

Public sentiment weighed heavily on the sentence, and the maximum term of ten-years for abduction and confinement was considered too light. Charges of stealing four camisoles worth 2,400 yen, which he gave to Fusako as gifts, were also included in Satō's sentencing, increasing the prison term to 14 years. He was sentenced on January 22, 2002.

Fusako's father was upset by the courts inability to enforce a harsher sentence. He released a statement at the conclusion of the trial:

"As parents, we are mortified by the existing situation . . . and cannot help feeling indignation about such a situation. Almost three years have passed since our daughter was released from the long confinement of nine years, two months and fifteen days. However, today's ruling fails to take account of the weight of the time passed for us and our daughter."

AFTERMATH

During his imprisonment, Nobuyuki Satō made a statement to a Japanese journalist: "The feelings of the weak are not worth considering. What else can they do but yield to the strong?"

Satō has spent 250 days in solitary confinement over ten years and makes continued complaints about the violation of his human rights.

Fusako Sano made some recovery, but her life has been difficult since her captivity. Reflecting on her past brings back painful memories. She has received on-going medical help and counselling. Fusako's legs regained their strength, and she enjoys long walks and photography. She works with her family on their rice paddies.

Her father died in 2007 after drowning in a favourite pond he would visit on walks with Fusako. She was with her father when he drowned.

Nobuyuki Satō will be eligible for release in 2016.

CHAPTER 10

ELIZABETH SMART

SANDY, UTAH – UNITED STATES.

2003

In the Western United States, two very different worlds collided. Wealth and poverty. Community and social outcasts. Clean living and depravity. An urgent call-to-arms ignited a desperate search for a kidnapped teenage girl in America's Mormon heartland.

LEAD UP TO CRIME

Brian David Mitchell preferred the name Immanuel, and followed what he believed was his divine path as a prophet. Wearing white robes and a long beard, he set out on a pilgrimage through the streets of Utah, preaching and helping the homeless.

Brian Mitchell came from a strict Mormon home, littered with familial mental illness and a father who housed his own prophetic delusions. At age 16, he was convicted for sexually exposing himself to a toddler and was sentenced to a juvenile detention centre.

After the break up of his first marriage, he kidnapped his two children and hid in New Hampshire, before returning them to the legal custody of their mother. Mitchell's second wife, Deborah, accused him of molesting their 18-month-old child and his two teenaged stepdaughters. The incidents were reported to police and to their church, but no action was taken by either organisation. Deborah also claimed the relationship was abusive and controlling.

Mitchell's all encapsulating religious fervour saw his two marriages fail. In 1985 he took a third wife, Wanda Eileen Barzee. Barzee was a manipulative and abusive woman, who turned away her children when they reached their teens. Her cruelty saw her serve up her unwitting children their pet rabbit for dinner.

Brian Mitchell and Wanda Barzee were members of the

Church of Jesus Christ of Latter-day Saints in Utah. After their increasingly bizarre behaviour and their fixation on Satanism, they were excommunicated in 2001. Now homeless for nearly a decade and begging on the streets, Mitchell and Barzee were known as an eccentric couple, nicknamed "Joseph and Mary" because of their robes. Barzee now adopted the name "God Adorneth."

Mitchell met Lois Smart and her daughter, Elizabeth, as he panhandled at Crossroads Plaza in Salt Lake City. Lois hired Mitchell to work around their yard, and fix their roof, for five hours in November 2001. It was then that he began formulating his plan to kidnap Elizabeth.

In preparation, Mitchell set up several campsites around Dry Creek Canyon, in order to hide out and remain mobile to avoid detection. His campsites contained hidden knives and holes dug in the ground to hide from thermal imaging helicopters and to use as campfires pit. One campsite contained an altar.

He believed it was God's will that he should take 49 additional wives, and Elizabeth would become his second. Seven months after his first visit to the Smart residence, Brian Mitchell returned.

HELD CAPTIVE

Elizabeth Smart was born into a wealthy Mormon family, the second of six children; her father a real estate and mortgage broker. In the early morning of June 5, 2002,

Mitchell used a garden chair to climb through the kitchen window of the Smart's home at 1509 Kristianna Circle, Federal Heights, Salt Lake City, Utah. He made his way to Elizabeth's bedroom, where he abducted the 14-year-old at knifepoint.

"I have a knife to your neck. Don't make a sound. Get up and come with me," Elizabeth recalled Mitchell saying.

Her frightened sister pretended to be asleep in the bed they shared. He marched Elizabeth six-and-a-half kilometres (4 miles) into the forest and to an established campsite. With the police quickly alerted to the abduction, the pair hid in bushes as a patrol car cruised passed.

At the campsite Mitchell burnt Elizabeth's red pyjamas, made her don white robes, and performed a wedding ceremony. Holding her down, Mitchell asked Barzee for confirmation, before raping Elizabeth.

For two months Elizabeth was tied to a tree and hidden under a lean-to constructed from branches. She was forced to remain naked and was raped daily. Elizabeth tried to escape but Mitchell dragged her back to the campsite, and told her an angel would cut her down if she made another escape attempt. He also threatened to kill her and her family. Believing Mitchell would murder her, Elizabeth requested her body be left out in the open, so her family would not think she had run away. Mitchell replied, "I'm not going to do that to you yet."

Despite the Mormon religion forbidding alcohol,

Mitchell forced Elizabeth to drink liquor and smoke marijuana with him several times a week. During these sessions she did not eat, to allow the intoxicants to have greater effect, so she would not be sober when he abused her, and to help her to forget.

A teacher had told Elizabeth's class that people who had premarital sex were likened to a piece of chewed gum. Elizabeth recalled the lecture in May 2013: "Imagine you're a stick of gum, and when you engage in sex, that is like being chewed. When you do that lots of times, you're going to become an old piece of gum. And who's going to want you after that?"

These words played on Elisabeth Smart's mind, creating doubt, making her fearful of returning home, believing people would treat the raped teen as a used piece of gum, and someone who now had no worth.

Dressed in robes that covered her entire body, except for her eyes, Elizabeth could be taken into public areas without being recognised. Elizabeth appeared hidden in plain sight, but always by the sides of her captors. Those who engaged with the trio were unable to identify Elizabeth. She lived on the streets of Utah with her captors: hungry, dirty, and encountering the homeless.

In August 2002, the trio were spotted at a Salt Lake City library after a member of the public recognised Elizabeth from her eyes. Detectives questioned Mitchell, but they failed to lift Elizabeth's veil, based on Mitchell's religious arguments. Barzee dug her nails into the desperate girl's leg until the detectives left.

The trio hitchhiked to California to avoid detection. They would remove their robes and Elizabeth would take on a disguise. Before they returned to Utah in March 2003, Mitchell was arrested twice, but police failed to make any link with the Smart case.

RESCUE

On March 11, 2003, Burger King employees called police to report a group of people harassing their customers, begging. After brief questioning, the trio were moved on.

The following day, March 12, 2003, two witnesses spotted Mitchell walking through the suburb of Sandy, Salt Lake City, recognising him from the intense publicity campaign based on a description provided by Elizabeth's sister. They didn't recognise Elizabeth as she was wearing sunglasses, a cheap wig, and a blue face veil. The trio were living off the street, carrying their own bedding and supplies. The witnesses called 911.

Elizabeth initially denied her own identity, but when questioned further, she answered, "If thou sayeth, I sayeth."

Elizabeth, now 15, had been missing for nine months.

Mitchell, 49, and Barzee, 57, were taken into custody. Their sun beaten faces were heavily lined and tanned from living on the streets. Their hair was long and scraggly, with

Mitchell's beard as wild as the man that kept it.

During an FBI interview Mitchell continually referred to the bible and his religious views, portraying himself as the Prophet Immanuel, which investigators called "bullshit," recognising Mitchell already had the intention to plead insanity.

Ed Smart, Elizabeth's father, took centre stage as media swarmed on the Smart's home with the news of her discovery. Within days Elizabeth was making her first media appearance, although she was coached not to reveal certain perverse details of the case, in order to prevent the voyeuristic media sensationalising her ordeal.

TRIAL

Police charged Mitchell and Barzee with aggravated kidnapping, aggravated sexual assault and aggravated burglary. But, on July 26, 2005, Mitchell was found to be mentally incompetent and unable to stand trial. The ruling was later overturned in 2009.

Barzee was first to stand trial. Neatly presented in a blue floral dress, with cardigan, glasses, and a bob of grey hair, Barzee looked every part of the typical grandmother. On November 17, 2009, she was sentenced to 15 years in prison. She is held at the Federal Medical Center, Carswell in Fort Worth, Texas. She is eligible for release in 2016.

Elizabeth was in France on a Mormon mission when Mitchell was brought to trial. She returned home for the trial commencement that finally began on November 8, 2010. It was the first time she had spoken publically about the intimate details of her abduction. Through a victim impact statement, Elizabeth confronted Mitchell in court. Mitchell didn't acknowledge Smart, but sat with his hands held in prayer and sung hymns. He had to be removed from the court when his singing became too loud.

On December 10, 2010, the jury found Brian David Mitchell guilty of kidnapping, and illegally transporting a minor across state lines for sexual purposes. On May 25, 2011, Mitchell was sentenced to life in prison without parole. He is currently housed in the United States Penitentiary, in Tucson, Arizona.

AFTERMATH

The Smart family has actively participated in large amounts of media, including interviews, books and film deals. The family has been criticised for cashing in on the publicity, and for only divulging certain aspects of the case. Many interviews show Elizabeth poised and articulate — growing frustrated by intrusive media questioning — Smart instead focusing on law reform and victim support.

Ed Smart still owns his real estate brokerage business, appears on television discussing abduction cases, and works full time as a motivational speaker.

Elizabeth married Matthew Gilmour in February 2012; she lives a fulfilling life, attends Brigham Young University in Utah, and is still devout to her faith. She and her family continue to do media interviews, engaging in public speaking to keep her story in the public eye. She works as a victims' advocate, supporting families of missing children through the Elizabeth Smart Foundation. She has also worked for ABC News in Utah, and Utah Congressman-elect and author Chris Stewart is co-writing her biography, due for release in late 2013.

CHAPTER 11

JOHN JAMELSKE

DEWITT, NEW YORK – UNITED STATES.

2003

Five women went missing while walking the streets of Syracuse, New York. Cruising around in his 1975 Mercury Comet, John Jamelske selected victims who could easily disappear into street life. With each victim he held captive, Jamelske was completing his most twisted collection. His crimes remained undetected for 15 years.

LEAD UP TO CRIME

The bunker in John Jamelske's backyard wasn't a secret. It had been constructed out in the open, with the help of hired contractors. Construction workers thought that building the bunker was strange — Jamelske explained the underground rooms would store his numerous collections — but two decades later its true purpose was revealed.

Jamelske was well known as a local eccentric, who walked around town in old clothes, collecting bottles for recycling. He collected many things, satisfying his appetite for compulsive hoarding. One collection included over 13,000 beer bottles from around the world. He filled his house and backyard with rubbish, and would eventually construct a 1.8 metre (6 foot) fence to keep the newly established neighbours from complaining.

Despite his unkempt appearance, Jamelske was a millionaire, miserly in nature, living off what others discarded. Jamelske originally owned a large area of land in the DeWitt countryside, living in a ranch-style house built in 1960, at 7070 Highbridge Road, DeWitt, New York. (Mailing addresses for the nearby town of Fayetteville extend into the neighbouring areas of DeWitt and Manlius, so the location of the property is often listed as Fayetteville.) Jamelske sub-divided his property, selling off parcels of land as the suburban outskirts encroached. He invested his money in real estate throughout the western United States and in casino developments.

The Jamelske children grew up and moved away, and his wife, Dorothy, lay confined to her bed, slowly dying. John Jamelske embarked on his most elaborate endeavour — a collection of females from different ethnic backgrounds.

HELD CAPTIVE

Kirsten

On September 17, 1988, Jamelske approached a 14-year-old Native American girl, who had been drinking with friends, as she walked along South Geddes Street, Syracuse. Convincing her to hop in his car, he drove her back to his house. Jamelske chained up the girl and kept her at the bottom of a disused well: leaving her naked, cold, and unable to escape. Kirsten would be Jamelske's first "friend."

Planning on keeping Kirsten for a longer stay, Jamelske embarked on building his dungeon. Hiring contractors attracted little attention from neighbours, who believed he was building a bomb shelter that reflected an aging man's Cold War paranoia. Machinery dug a giant hole, concrete walls were built, and solid steel doors were fixed in place. Two bare rooms formed an underground prison.

To force Kirsten to submit to him, Jamelske threatened to kill her family, showing her photographs of her younger brother. Rapes became daily features, but Jamelske's view of Kirsten was changing. He considered himself to be in a relationship with his captive: bringing her gifts, playing games, and praying together. He made her send a series of letters and recordings back to her parents, to confuse her whereabouts for anyone searching for her.

After three years, Jamelske decided to end Kirsten's captivity. Driven to the airport by Jamelske's son, Brian, the frail girl was taken to California on a ten-day vacation. Afterwards she was flown home, returning unaccompanied, where she didn't tell anyone of her ordeal.

Michelle

On March 31, 1995, Jamelske completed the first stage of his new cycle, cruising the streets, stalking victims, and finding out where they lived. Michelle, a Latino girl of 14, already had a history of running away and drug abuse. Pulling up beside her near Lodi and Catherine Street, Syracuse, Jamelske offered her money to deliver a package — all she had to do was retrieve it from his basement. The runaway accepted the offer.

Jamelske ordered Michelle into the basement to collect the package. He trapped her in the darkness, returning to force-feed her pills. She woke to find herself chained to a wall. He threatened her family, while showing her their photographs. He took Viagra as the onslaught of abuse began.

In the early days, Michelle attacked her captor as she

attempted to fend him off. He humiliated the constrained girl by taking naked photographs of her. He also told her he was part of a syndicate that sold girls into sex slavery. A bath was brought down, but the bunker had no plumbing. Michelle was hosed down once a week, the water draining onto the floor to evaporate, causing mould to grow in the dungeon.

Nearly two years later, Jamelske decided to release Michelle. In that time she had been allowed outside, into the backyard, just once. Jamelske encouraged her to return to school and make peace with her mother. He gave her a bag of marijuana as a parting gift, and drove her home.

Michelle didn't make a report to police, afraid of retribution. She had been reported missing at the time of her disappearance, but police believed the case was simply another runaway or drug related. Jamelske continued to stalk her home for some time afterwards.

Tina

Jamelske was back on the streets, scouring for his next victim on August 30, 1997. As 52-year-old mother of two, Tina, walked alone along John Street, Syracuse, home to an Asian community, Jamelske pulled up along side the Vietnamese woman. Breaking from his *modus operandi,* he dragged Tina into his car, and diverted to an abandoned house where he raped her. During the attack he slapped Tina on her left ear, causing her to become partially deaf.

Jamelske transported Tina back to his DeWitt dungeon the next day, by binding and gagging her and stuffing her in a cardboard box. In the bunker she suffered the same fate as his previous two captives; she was chained, visited daily, and raped. Tina spoke little English and communicated with her captor through pointing at pictures she cut out from magazines and glued to the wall. Over time Jamelske taught her how to speak new words.

While held captive, Jamelske forced her to sing a cappella as he sat and listened. He bought her a television so they could watch evangelical programs together, and made her perform repetitive meaningless chores. The woman slept on a wooden platform. Jamelske placed a life-sized plastic skeleton on a mat next to her bed, so it could watch her as she slept.

"I did everything he asked, hoping he would release me. I did not want to die down there in those rooms because no one would ever find my body and my soul would remain in a cold place," Tina wrote in a statement read by police.

After Jamelske decided he had had enough sex with Tina, he dropped her off at a bus stop on May 23, 1998, and gave her $50. She reported the ordeal to police, but they didn't believe her, yelling at her and telling her she was lying. No meaningful investigation was conducted.

Dorothy Jamelske died on August 2, 1999, during one of her husband's quiet periods, but he was soon out hunting.

Jennifer

On the spring night of May 11, 2001, three years after the release of Jamelske's last captive, he spotted Jennifer, 26, a Caucasian mother of two, walking along Geddes Street, Syracuse. She was drunk and had taken drugs. She was on her way to a friend's house when she accepted a ride from Jamelske. She claimed there was a gang of kids nearby, harassing her and making her feel nervous. The skies threatened with rain.

Jennifer recalls driving into Jamelske's garage and trying to exit the car, and then her memory failed. She later woke in the dungeon. When Jamelske came for her, she was naked in the darkness and put up a fight. In retribution, he beat her, and burnt her on the back with a cigar, which would later form into an abscess.

Jamelske told Jennifer that he planned to sell her over the internet to a sex slave syndicate for $30,000. From the markings and graffiti on the walls, she wondered if other females had been held captive in the dungeon before. She contemplated suicide. He allowed her to write a letter to her family, telling them she was in rehab, finally addressing her long-standing drug problem. He tortured her as he did with the other females, and read her verses of the bible.

On July 7, Jennifer was released after only two months. She was blindfolded and dropped off in front of her mother's house. She made a report to police, who took her details. Jennifer described Jamelske's 1974 Mercury Comet, but police failed to find the vehicle. Had police broadened their search even slightly, they would have discovered that Jamelske's car was actually a 1975 model.

Police refused to believe Jennifer's claims of being held captive, relying on the letter stating she had gone to rehab. "They thought I was making it up or something," said Jennifer.

The case was made inactive.

Meikka

Again, cruising the streets of Syracuse in mid-October 2002, Jamelske spotted a 16-year-old African-American runaway at corner of Elk and South Salina Streets. He took her back to his house, locked her up, raped her, and named her "Meikka."

Jamelske reinforced the story that he belonged to a sex slave syndicate, and told her vicious dogs guarded the dudgeon, ready to attack her if she attempted an escape. He made promises of release dates, which he never granted, explaining the syndicate would not allow her freedom until she had more sex with him.

Of all Jamelske's "friends," Meikka was who he found himself drawn closest to, allowing her the greatest freedom. With his wife now deceased, Jamelske was free to transform his filth-ridden house into a makeshift prison. He boarded up windows, using refrigerator shelves as bars, and covering windows with plywood. Meikka slept next to him in his bed and used the house toilet, rather than a bucket like the previous captives. With his growing confidence, Jamelske was ready to take their relationship further. Outside.

In April 2003, Jamelske began taking Meikka on shopping trips, bowling, and to karaoke bars where she sang on stage, but he was always by her side, watching her. During an outing at a recycling station on April 8, 2003, Meikka managed to talk him into allowing her to make a phone call to check church service times. She phoned her sister for help, which consequently led her sister to call 911. To not raise suspicion of her actions, Meikka left with her captor.

Police tracked Jamelske down and he was soon arrested.

AFTERMATH

Jamelske was originally charged with kidnapping, rape and sodomy.

Behind the high fence surrounding his DeWitt house, police discovered a bizarre three metre (10 foot) cross in the front yard with chains dangling from the cross beams, and on top was fixed a replica of a human head.

For his crimes, Jamelske expected a community service order or a brief period in prison and took a plea bargain. He pleaded guilty and was convicted of five counts of kidnapping. On July 14, 2003, John Jamelske was sentenced to 18-years to life and imprisoned at Clinton Correctional Facility in Dannemora, New York.

"I'm just truly sorry for what I did. I've had a lot of time to think about it and I'm just sorry for what I did and how it's affected everyone and God bless all of them," Jamelske stated to the court.

In reality, Jamelske remained mostly unrepentant for his crimes, deluded to the trauma and lifelong damage he had done to his victims. He still believed that his captives were his friends, that he was helping them, and that if they had the choice they would have chosen to be in relationships with him.

The women return to live as close-to-normal lives as they could. Some victims appeared in media interviews, telling of the ongoing trauma of being held captive in the dungeon and used as sex slaves. In court, Kirsten's cousin stated that she believed the victims should be able to torture Jamelske, the same as he did to them.

In 2005 the DeWitt house was sold for $100,000. Jamelske's assets, believed to be worth up to several million dollars, were liquidated and divided amongst his five victims.

John Jamelske will be eligible for parole in 2021, when he is 86.

CAPTIVE HUMANS

CHAPTER 12

NATASHA RYAN

ROCKHAMPTON, QUEENSLAND - AUSTRALIA.

2003

Females began disappearing around Rockhampton, Queensland, in August 1998. In less than a year "The Rockhampton Rapist" had struck fear into the quiet community as five local females were abducted, raped and murdered. Leonard John Fraser was charged and brought to trial, but as the evidence played out in court, the case took a startling twist.

100

THE ROCKHAMPTON RAPIST

Leonard John Fraser spent much of his adult life behind bars. Illiterate, Fraser left school at 14, and within a year was court ordered to live at Gosford Boys' Home in New South Wales, after he was caught stealing. Once released, he graduated to robbery, assault, car theft, and rape. He lived off the proceeds earned by prostitutes, and had numerous homosexual affairs. In 1974, he was found guilty of a string of rapes across Sydney, after attacking at least four women, and was sentenced to 22 years in prison. He was released after seven years, and immediately fell back into crime. He committed more rapes and sexual offences, and served at least another two stays in prison. Each time he was released, he set out to commit similar crimes. He was also known to have sex with dogs.

On August 31, 1998, Natasha Ryan, 14, went missing after her mother dropped her off in front of her high school. She had previously run away and had been experimenting with drugs. Fraser confessed to murdering Ryan on a farm where he later buried her body beneath a mango tree.

On December 28, 1998, Julie Dawn Turner, 39, disappeared after leaving Rockhampton's Airport Liberties nightclub. She was in an abusive relationship and was planning on leaving her boyfriend. She had briefly worked with Fraser at a local abattoir.

On March 1, 1999, Beverley Doreen Leggo, 36, was

doing her banking in Rockhampton when she vanished. She was reported missing by her landlord, and her handbag was found on the banks of the Fitzroy River. She too was in a volatile relationship.

On April 18, 1999, Sylvia Maria Benedetti, 19, a drug user and a "street wanderer" was last seen sitting beside Leonard Fraser on a bench in Rockhampton Mall.

On April 22, 1999, Keyra Steinhardt, 9, was abducted, raped and murdered in broad daylight as she walked home from school. Her parents had only recently allowed the girl to walk home alone.

Given the name of "The Rockhampton Rapist," Leonard Fraser appeared at his first trial for his crimes against Keyra Steinhardt. He received an indefinite life sentence on November 9, 2000. Besides being previously imprisoned for other rape offences, he also confessed to killing a series of women in further unsolved cases. Collections of ponytails were found at Fraser's apartment from women that could not be identified. He confessed to multiple crimes and murders spanning over 30 years. If all the confessions were true, he would be one of the worst serial killers in Australia's history.

Fraser was further charged with the murders of the other four females who had gone missing since 1988. Three of the victim's remains had been found, and he was suspected in another three disappearances. His second murder trial began at the start of April 2003.

LEAD UP TO CRIME

Natasha Ryan had a history of being a troubled teen, experimenting with drugs, suspended from school, and slashing her wrists for which she received counselling. She had tried to run away twice before, though the reasons why are not clear. Before her disappearance, Ryan hinted to a friend that she was planning on going into hiding, but had concerns she would get her boyfriend into trouble. On both previous occasions she stayed with her 22-year-old boyfriend, milk deliveryman, Scott Angus Black. Black had previously dated Ryan's older sister.

In 2002, convicted child killer, Leonard John Fraser, was charged with Natasha Ryan's murder. The Rockhampton community held a memorial service in her honour.

HELD CAPTIVE

Desperate for affection, Natasha ran away and decided to hide with her boyfriend. Police investigated Scott Black for several months after Natasha's disappearance, and twice during police interviews he denied knowing of her whereabouts. Ryan spent her captivity inside a house in the coastal town of Yeppoon, 43 kilometres (27 miles) north of Rockhampton, in a house that sported views of the southern Great Barrier Reef.

Natasha was not held against her will, but rather served a self-imposed captivity. She spent five years peering through the curtains of a rather unimpressive house, looking out to a world that she could no longer be part of. Her only connection with the outside world was her boyfriend. Occasionally at night he would drive her to the beach where he would let her wade around. On the journey, which only took a few minutes, Ryan hid on the floor of his ute. She was never allowed to go out during daylight hours, not even onto the veranda.

During this time the couple moved to 346 Mills Avenue, North Rockhampton. Washing never hung on the line. Neighbours claimed Scott Black was abusive when they asked him to turn down his music, and he threatened he would charge them with trespass if they came on to his property to complain again. His neighbours also noticed that there were no lights on at night, and Black had a very limited social life. His family brought over large amounts of food. Even though the neighbours routinely settled on their veranda, they never saw Natasha and simply thought Black was a "private person."

Ryan spent her days playing video games and sewing. She watched on television as police searched for her body.

DISCOVERY

On the ninth day of Leonard Fraser's murder trial the hearing took a dramatic turn when he was cleared of her murder. On April 10, 2003, Natasha Ryan herself, now 18, appeared in the witness box.

As the trial against Fraser had progressed, Rockhampton Police received an anonymous note. It read: "Natasha Ryan is alive and well," it also contained Black's phone number. Police attended Black's house to summons him to appear in court as a witness. While inside Black's house, police noticed his nervous behaviour when they approached the bedroom. An officer found Ryan hiding in a cupboard, where she hid during the regular visits made by Black's family. When discovered, Ryan looked pale, as though she was suffering from a terminal illness.

Natasha Ryan's family believed she had been murdered. She begged her mother for forgiveness after being missing for four-and-a-half years.

The Australian and international media pursued Ryan, with television station Channel Nine offering to pay her $200,000 for an exclusive interview. Talks soon began of making her story into a movie, which never eventuated.

TRIAL

Ryan and Black were both committed to stand trial, charged with causing a false police investigation. Searchers had spent over $500,000 looking for her body, and burnt large tracks of bushland in the search. Police also sought to be repaid costs for their $151,000 investigation.

The trial lasted a month and involved more than 100 witnesses. In her defence, Ryan stated it was not her responsibility to let police know she was alive, despite knowing another person was on trial for her murder. Ryan was fined $1,000 but received no conviction. She was not ordered to repay police costs, due to her inability to pay, and because of her young age when the crime was committed.

Scott Black was found guilty of perjury, for lying on the stand at Leonard Fraser's committal hearing; stating he had no contact with Ryan, and she wasn't living at his house. He was fined $3,000, ordered to pay police costs of $16,740, and jailed for 12 months.

AFTERMATH

In 2008, the pair was married in front of 35 guests by a celebrant, and the Australian magazine *Woman's Day* paid $200,000 for the couples wedding photos. They have three children together.

The effects of Ryan's self-imposed captivity has caused her to become further isolated, fearful of scorn and attack from Rockhampton residents, upset over the controversy.

Ryan has stuck true to her vow never to disclose the reason why she ran away to live with Black, though it is believed Ryan may have been pregnant and suffering depression, according to police.

"I'm never going to say publicly why I left," she told another Australian women's magazine. "I know why I left. I'm not sure my mum and my sister completely know all the reasons. I'm not sure it would make any difference saying why I left — I feel whatever I say wouldn't be good enough for the pain I've caused my family."

Ryan is studying to become a nurse and now goes by the name Tash Black.

In 2011, Black appeared in Rockhampton Magistrates Court and pleaded guilty to refusing police a breath test. Police were called to his house after a reported drunken argument over moving a vehicle to the garage. Black lost his job as a milk deliveryman after his license was suspended.

Leonard Fraser received a further three indefinite life sentences. He suffered a heart attack at Wolston Correctional Centre in Richlands, Queensland, on December 26, 2006. He died in hospital on New Year's Day 2007, aged 55.

CHAPTER 13

VICTOR MOKHOV

SKOPIN, RYAZAN OBLAST — RUSSIA.

2004

The nightmare that Alexander Komin concocted in Vyatskiye Polyany was reborn, continuing five years after his death. A new chapter of terror would begin, just over 1,000 kilometres (620 miles) to the southwest, in a town half the size. A man desperate to father children embarked on a copycat crime, in a country that had become blind to the plight of its fellow citizens.

LEAD UP TO CRIME

Victor Mokhov (Виктор Мохов), 50, lived in Skopin, in western Russia, located 248 kilometres (154 miles) southeast of Moscow. Mokhov was a thin, unassuming man, respected by his workmates, neighbours, and police. He held a position as a communist party member and army officer before the collapse of the Soviet Union. He was a college graduate, completing a degree as a "Mountain Master," allowing him to work in the local mines. But, as the mines closed around Skopin, and workers moved away, Mokhov decided to remain behind and gained employment at an automotive factory.

Mokhov lived all his life with his mother, marrying in 1979, but the marriage lasted only three months. His mother described him as fearful of women, a man who was easily dumped in the relationship. His father had been jailed for rape. Watching a documentary about Alexander Komin, a fellow Russian who kept slaves in an underground prison, Mokhov was inspired to also take female slaves.

Mokhov constructed his own bunker under the garage at the rear of his mother's overgrown property. He called it his harem. For approximately three years he worked throughout the night, excavating around 60 tons of soil. He sealed the two-and-a-half metre by three-metre (8 x 10 foot) cellar behind three doors.

A sheet metal door, held by magnets on the side of the

rust coloured garage, concealed the entrance; a screwdriver was used to pry it open. The second door was on a platform a couple of feet down. The cellar had two rooms. A homemade ladder dropped to a small holding room. A small safe-like door, several inches thick and held by a large padlock, opened to the main chamber, which would be the living quarters of his victims.

He fitted the concrete walled room with bunk beds, a heater, a cooking element and a bucket for a toilet. An electric ventilator pumped oxygen into the dungeon.

In December 1999, Mokhov kidnapped a 16-year-old girl after getting her drunk. She fled the property after refusing his sexual advances. He followed her, hit her over the head, and dragged her into his cellar. The girl escaped two weeks later, but didn't report the crime.

Mokhov had greater plans. He wanted to keep many women for up to 20 years, providing him with ten children each.

"I wanted to have lots of children, I wanted to improve the demographic situation in Russia," said Mokhov.

HELD CAPTIVE

On September 30, 2000, Katya Martynova, 14, and Lena Simakhina, 17, left an open-air disco in Ryazan, the administrative centre of Ryazan Oblast. They were celebrating *Vyara, Nadezhda and Lyubov,* an Eastern Orthodox Church festival for Sophia's three daughters -

Hope, Faith and Love. Lena and Katya were acquaintances and decided to attend the street party together.

Afterwards, while the girls waited for a bus, Mokhov pulled along side and offered them a ride. The girls accepted — offering lifts in Russia is a cultural practice, with drivers feeling obliged to help others if possible. A female accomplice, Yelena Badukina, assisted Mokhov. Mokhov had waited for Badukina while she served a prison sentence for murdering a lover, but his plans for their relationship dissolved when she was released and went with a lesbian lover instead. As compensation, Badukina agreed to help capture substitute females to fulfil Movhov's desires. She travelled in the car with Mokhov to Ryazan.

Mokhov laced vodka with a sedative and offered it to the girls, who felt it would be rude not to drink it. It rendered the girls defenceless. He drove them to his home in Skopin, 126 kilometres (78 miles) south of Ryazan.

Mokhov first raped Katya on a bed in the main section of the garage that night. He locked her alone in the cellar while he raped Lena. Mokhov then asked Lena to fetch Katya from the cellar, when she went inside, he locked them both in. A regime of abuse was established over the following weeks.

The holding room walls were covered with pornographic pictures. Mokhov showed sexual positions from an instructional booklet, and then raped the girls individually in the tiny room. He kept notes about his views on sex. "Older animals (like dogs and cats) are rejuvenated by having sex with younger ones. That is true with humans, too."

The girls endured daily rapes, forming part of their repetitive dungeon lives. He starved the girls and left them constantly fearing for their lives. Resisting Mokhov resulted in the electricity being cut off, leaving the girls in darkness, without heat or light. The oxygen pump would also be cut off.

The cellar contained a bunk bed, though the teens shared the lower mattress, holding each other for comfort. Religious symbols decorated the walls, along with cartoon characters (one painting of a wolf choking a rabbit), and posters of pop stars.

A month into their captivity, Lena and Katya attacked Mokhov in a bid to escape, attempting to strangle him with a heater cord. He was too strong for the pair.

Because of the harsh conditions, Katya's puberty was suppressed, saving her from the torment Lena would endure. Lena gave birth to a boy, Vladik, on November 6, 2001. Mokhov provided the girls with a 1942 medical book to instruct them on birthing. He took the baby from the cellar. On June 6, 2003, Lena gave birth to a second boy, Oelg. At four months old he became ill and was removed from the cellar. Mokhov changed the baby's clothes and found several concealed notes, before dumping the child on the doorstep of a local house.

Mokhov allowed certain elements of the outside world in, rewarding the girl's obedient behaviour: pens, magazines, paper, books, paints, music, and a black and white television. Katya spent her time working on an extraordinary collection of detailed paintings.

Neighbours noticed Mokhov's mother buying an unusual amount of food, too much just for her and Victor, but they didn't question it. They had also seen Victor entering the hatch on the side of the garage, but believed he was storing potatoes for his mother.

RESCUE

Police had given up looking for Lena Simakhina and Katya Martynova, believing they had been murdered. Victor Mokhov became more brazen, briefly allowing the girls to experience the outside world, taking them out into the garden in the spring of 2003.

Katya managed to gain Mokhov's trust, and he involved her in a plan to enslave a medical student, Alena Pestova, who rented a room from him. As Katya posed as his niece, she slipped the student a note. A report was made to the police station situated less than a kilometre away.

Police arrived at Mokhov's mother's house on May 4, 2004. Victor attempted to run out the backdoor, but was captured by police.

Police videotaped the rescue. They called out to the girls, "We're coming."

Lena sat on the edge of the bunk, her hands folded, eight months pregnant. She called out, "Don't film us."

"Be quiet," the police replied.

Katya emerged from the underground prison clutching a castle made from matchsticks. The girls could barely walk and rested against trees in the garden.

The pair had been held captive for three years, eight months, and four days.

TRIAL

On May 6, 2004, Victor Mokhov appeared in the Skopin City Court and he was ordered to return to his mother's property and walk police and officials over the scene. He explained his crimes as his confessions were recorded on video.

Mokhov attempted to convince the court (and the girls) that he took good care of them, feeding them and bringing them gifts. Lena and Katya appeared in court, hiding behind their parents as Mokhov launched a tirade about all he had done for them.

Victor Mokhov was charged with the abduction of two or more persons, and with rape of a minor. He received a sentence of 17 years, to be served in a high-security Siberian labour camp.

"Nothing is enough for him," said Lena.

For her role in the crime Yelena Badukina was sentenced to five-and-a-half years imprisonment. In May

2007, Badukina allegedly fell into a sewage pit while drunk, where she drowned.

AFTERMATH

The residents of Skopin descended upon the house, and broke all the windows, causing Mokhov's mother to board the windows and barricade herself inside.

By the time they were rescued, Lena's babies had been adopted, and she did not seek to find them. She couldn't recognise the babies as hers, but as rather something placed inside her by Mokhov. The baby she carried when rescued was stillborn.

In 2008 Lena and Katya decided to return to the cellar in Skopin with a UK documentary crew for Channel 5. Both girls appeared apprehensive as they approached the garage.

"Oh, what a nightmare," said Lena.

Scared of going inside, the girls feared what was down the homemade ladders. The holding room and cellar were as they were left four years ago when the girls were rescued, except decay had set in, repealing the past. The cellar seemed like a different place, smaller, and they had forgotten many things since their rescue. Instead of the negative emotions they were expecting, the girls found the experience cathartic.

"I'm really glad we did it. We both are," said Lena.

Both women made remarkable recoveries, and are both

married. They have rejected psychological help, instead choosing not to see themselves as victims. Lena studied to become a teacher and hopes to have four children. She celebrates May 4, the anniversary of their rescue, as her second birthday. Katya decided to forgo art school after not being able to afford the tuition. Publishers rejected a book of 321 poems written while she was held captive.

CHAPTER 14

ANNAPURNA SAHU

DHENKANAL, ORISSA - INDIA.

2005

Annapurna Sahu waited as the world passed by. The career and marriage she had dreamed of in her youth did not arrive. Instead, outside the walls of her dank confines, faint sounds pushed their way in, letting her know that life was continuing on without her in a world that was only an impossible step away.

LEAD UP TO CRIME

The Sahu family are the wealthy owners of a flourmill in the small city of Dhenkanal, population of 57,000, located in India's east. Their daughter, Annapurna, had left school after completing the seventh grade. At the age of 18, she was training to become a midwife when her ordeal begun.

Annapurna's family committed her to an arranged marriage with a widower from the nearby village of Indupur. When Annapurna turned down the offer, it was that day her parents decided she was mentally unstable. First she was taken to doctors for a diagnosis and cure. Doctors could not diagnose any ailments, a fact confirmed by her brother, Ganeswar Sahu. Annapurna was then taken to witch doctors, ending with similar results. Not obtaining the diagnosis they desired, the family took treatment into their own hands.

The Sahu family claimed Annapurna was acting out with "wild behaviour." Her father, Brajabandhu Sahu, claimed she constantly tore off her clothing, defecated everywhere and began attacking neighbours.

HELD CAPTIVE

Around 1980, Annapurna Sahu was locked in a small shed at the back of the family home. Annapurna's outhouse consisted of a brick lean-to, constructed in the corner of an unkempt backyard. The outhouse had the dimensions of an outside toilet, barely a few feet in length and covered by a shoddy tin roof held down by pieces of wood. The scene was in stark contrast to the lavish lifestyle the family had awarded upon themselves. Squatting on a dirt floor, Annapurna spent her years in a brick and asbestos outhouse barely high enough to stand up in.

Her mother, Yashonda Sahu, claimed Annapurna had torn up the floorboards of her tiny room.

"She kept running away here and there. So I kept her confined," said her father.

Her family claimed that she had been fed and given plenty of water. She tore her clothes, so they refused to give her anymore. She slept and defecated in a small pot in the corner of her confinement. During captivity her hair turned grey. Annapurna barely spoke a word to anyone and lost most of her capacity for language.

RESCUE

In early September 2005, a concerned neighbour finally made a pilgrimage to the local police station in the Gopabandhu Bazar area of Dhenkanal, India. It was a short journey they had held off making for many years. Police conducted an investigation in front of a band of growing onlookers. Inside a tiny outhouse they found a naked woman, her posture crumpled, her hair stripped grey by the years, her face carved with the look of blank resignation.

Police officials maintained Annapurna, now 43, had

been held captive for 25 years, while her father claimed she had been locked away for only four years. Annapurna's captivity had managed to avoid detection by law enforcement, despite Dhenkanal's two police stations being located on either side of the Sahu's house.

When a female police officer broke into the room she found Annapurna huddled, naked and emaciated, trying to understand what was going on.

Anna showed no sign of mental illness when rescued. Her family stated that she was "aggressive and unbalance," though police thought she appeared "normal" and could answer simple and direct questions. Professionals who looked after Annapurna have not substantiated the Sahu's family claims of mental illness or "wild behaviour."

Due to Annapurna's low haemoglobin level and malnutrition, she required a blood transfusion to regain strength. Guards were assigned at the hospital to protect her from the media onslaught, provided by Dayananda Saraswati Service Mission.

At the hospital her brother admitted that he thought his sisters wild behaviour would put off his potential suitors and his own chances at securing a bride.

CHARGES

Neighbours had reported Annapurna a number of times, though according to the police, it was a family matter. Abuse towards females is often ignored in India. When women hit a state of depression, they are often shunned by their families, or sent to state run hospitals. The penalties for keeping people held captive in India is minimal compared to other areas of the world.

Section 341 of the Indian Penal Code states:

> "341. Punishment for wrongful restraint. -- Whoever wrongfully restrains any person shall be punished with simple imprisonment for a term which may extend to one month, or with fine which may extend to five hundred rupees, or with both."

Police decided not to press charges.

"It's good that she was locked up by her family members. What other option did her father have other than keeping her in a room? It would have been no good had she run away from home and then got raped," said Debadutta Pradhan, the officer in charge of Dhenkanal police station, when he spoke to the Indian media. "After all he is the woman's father."

AFTERMATH

The Sahu's stated they were upset over the handling of the investigation as it had brought shame to the family name, although they were cautiously aware to thank the high ranking local law administration for coming to Annapurna's aid.

Once Annapurna was rescued, her doctor said she showed signs of improvement, and was later removed to a rehabilitation centre by the magistrate. She was handed over to the Non-Government Organisation Dayananda Saraswati Mission and the Red Cross paid for her treatment.

As a way of distancing herself from her past, she now requests she be called Purna. Purna continued to make her recovery, provided by an old age facility. She quickly regained her speech, but only in patches and would tire easily.

She doesn't like to talk about her decades long captivity. "The past is past. Why talk about it?" Talking about the past makes her cry.

Purna was eventually released back into the care of her family.

SIMILAR CASE - NAROTTAM SETHY

One year after Annapurna Sahu was liberated, another captive was found being held by their family in a nearby village. In September 2006, Narottam Sethy, 42, was released in Koshala village, Orissa, located approximately 70 kilometres (44 miles) northeast from where Annapurna Sahu had been discovered. He had been held captive for 15 years, after he turned mad from being rejected by his first love.

"Having been frustrated in love, Narottam turned violent and always made bids to hurt the villagers," said his mother, Abala Sethy. "His erratic behaviour was unbearable and hence we confined him to a room for the safety of the family and others. He used to throw away and break utensils and other household articles after he turned mad. We did not have any other way than restricting his physical movement."

Narottam Sethy was held in a three-metre by three-metre (10 x 10 foot) locked room, with walls lined with mud. His sanitary conditions were similar to Annapurna's. Once released, Narottam required medical attention and was removed to a state care hospital.

Police were alerted to his captivity when it was reported in a local newspaper.

CHAPTER 15

TANYA KACH

MCKEESPORT, PENNSYLVANIA — UNITED STATES.

2006

A storm was brewing over McKeesport. Tanya Kach rose from obscurity when she claimed she was held captive in a bedroom for ten years. She claimed she was hidden away in a rust belt home, in the industrial wasteland of a former steel town, in an area surrounded by abandoned houses and decaying steel mills. Doubt quickly crept into the minds of many when Tanya's story unfolded, and people wondered if she was truly held against her will.

LEAD UP TO CRIME

Tanya Kach, 14, struggled with her parent's divorce. Sherri Kach (née Koehnke) worked at McDonalds. Mentally disturbed, she suffered from breakdowns and allegedly threatened her daughter with a knife. The conflict between mother and daughter escalated, which saw Sherri Kach bring a restraining order against Tanya. The girl was placed in the sole custody of her father.

In April 1995 Jerry (Jerald) Kach, butcher, met Jo-Ann McGuire. He separated from his wife. Within months Jerry and Tanya moved in with Jo-Ann in McKeesport, on the outskirts of Pittsburgh, Pennsylvania. The dysfunctional household was in a constant state of turmoil, with fights frequently erupting and Tanya running away. Tanya perceived Jo-Ann as the enemy, believing she was turning her birth parents against her.

In September 1995 Tanya started at Cornell Middle School in McKeesport. She was socially isolated, with no close friends, and her classmates knew very little about her. She caused trouble and was often involved in fights, being summoned to the principal's office. She quickly drew the attention of security guard Thomas Hose, 38, who presented himself around school as a "kingpin of the women," often flirting with female students.

Thomas Hose was employed as a security guard through a private firm, St. Mortiz Security Services Inc., in 1994. The firm contracted Hose to work at the school to monitor the schoolyard and break up fights.

Hose lived in a two-bedroom weatherboard home at 1002 Soles Street, McKeesport, with his elderly parents, Eleanor and Howard. Hose shared an upstairs bedroom with his 12-year-old son, Justin.

Hose would often pull Tanya out of class under the guise of disciplinary action. The more trouble Tanya caused, the more she was pulled out of class. Hose would escort Tanya through the hallways, giving the impression she was being taken to the principals office to be chastised. Hose would use these opportunities to allow the teen to confide in him. They often rendezvoused under a gym stairwell, where they would spend their time kissing. Other students noticed Hose and Kach acting flirtatiously and suspected they had formed a relationship.

Tanya's wayward behaviour saw Cornell Middle School on the verge of expelling her. Out of options on how to control his daughter, Jerry Kach readied himself to appear before a judge, to present an application to make Tanya a Ward of the State, which could have seen her housed in a juvenile detention centre.

The eighth-grader believed neither parent, nor her stepmother, loved or wanted her. Tanya wrote in her diary that she was in love with Tom. She spent Super Bowl Sunday at his house on January 28, 1996, where their sexual relationship developed.

Kach packed a rucksack and on February 10, 1996, and

she went voluntarily to Hose's house. She entered his bedroom, where she claimed she remained for four years.

Judith Sokol, then 48, hairdresser, assisted Hose when Tanya ran away. She let Tanya into her home, and cut and dyed her hair. It was claimed Tom and Tanya had sex in Sokol's home, a claim Sokol denied, stating she prevented the act from occurring.

HELD CAPTIVE

Jerry Kach filed a missing-persons report with McKeesport police four days after Tanya ran away, on February 14. It was the fourth report he had filed in recent months, as Tanya had run away on multiple occasions, so he didn't see the urgency of contacting police, feeling he was being a bother to them. Jo-Ann stated she was "glad she was gone because of all the problems she caused," and that Tanya was setting a bad example for her seven year-old son. Jerry continued to look for Tanya around the streets of McKeesport, but his contact with police would remain scant.

Tanya claimed Tom Hose's attitude changed towards her after she moved in, and he threatened her life to prevent her from leaving. Police visited the Hose residence, but failed to find Kach, who hid in the basement at the time.

Hose continued working at the middle school, and Tanya locked the bedroom door from the inside when he left for work. No physical restraints were used, but Kach claimed she was "brainwashed" into staying. Justin Hose never informed his grandparents about the girl who slept on his side of the bed, while he slept on the floor in a sleeping bag.

During the day, Tanya spent her time watching television and sitting on the bed, waiting for Hose to come home. A bucket in the corner was her toilet. Once a week she was taken to the basement to shower while Hose's parents were out. Hose brought food up to the room, and gave her gifts of money and jewellery. She hid in the closet when Hose's parents came to the bedroom door.

Hose had sex with the underage girl. Justin was usually out of the room or asleep when his father had sex with Tanya. She recorded her sexual encounters with Hose on a calendar, which she claimed Hose would take to school at the end of each year, so he could brag to his workmates about how much sex he was having.

The crime-riddled area of McKeesport had amassed a growing list of runaways. Police knew Tanya for previously going missing and for her truancy. Her disappearance quickly fell off the radar. Her family rarely contacted police to check the status of the investigation into her disappearance.

On July 6, 1998, Kimberly Krimm, 14, was found murdered in a nearby cemetery. Police suspected Tanya could have been murdered as part of a serial killing, and they released her photo nationwide. Her image would appear on a reported 400,000,000 milk cartons, Kach claimed. A record of the true number of the milk cartons printed, or their existence, has not been substantiated.

At age 18, Tanya was allowed out of the house, leaving while Hose's parents were not at home. She used the alias Nikki Allen. Hose provided her with a cell phone and cash.

In Tanya's final year at the Hose house, Tom pretended to move her in, and introduced her to his parents. Hose proposed. Kach accepted, flashing her ring to friends. She went shopping with Eleanor Hose, attended church, and spent her days hanging out with friends. She moved freely about McKeesport, spending her days at JJ's Deli Mart, located just down the street on Versailles Avenue.

ESCAPE

On March 21, 2006, after Tanya had been hanging around JJ's Deli Mart for ten months, she told owner Joe Sparico, "If you go to a website for missing children, you will see a picture of me there."

A few hours later multiple police cars arrived at the Hose residence. Tanya was located approximately 2.4 kilometres (1.5 miles) from where her father and stepmother lived. Tanya Kach was now 24 years old. She came out of her captivity with bleach blonde hair, manicured nails, wearing jewellery, and immaculately dressed. Within hours of her discovery she made her first media interview.

Hose, now 48 years old, was arrested and taken in for questioning.

Justin Hose, 22, had moved out of Soles Street at 18. He was questioned by police but soon released, explaining he had been told not to tell anyone about the girl sharing the bedroom.

"She never claimed she was held captive," Police Chief Joseph Pero told the Pittsburgh Post-Gazette. "I think it was more of a mental thing. He used threats. If she left, he would kill her, from what she says."

Many people doubted Tanya's story, reporting to have previously met Kach and that she appeared well kept and friendly.

"Stockholm syndrome, my ass," said Debbie Carney, the neighbour from across the street.

"Honestly?" said a former classmate. "I didn't know she was missing until she was found."

However, as the spotlight moved onto the Kach case, Tanya constantly reinforced the claims that Hose, in fact, held her captive.

TRIAL

Thomas Hose was charged with involuntary deviate sexual intercourse with a minor, aggravated indecent assault, statutory sexual assault, interfering with the custody of a child, corruption of a minor, and child endangerment. No charges were made against Hose for kidnapping or holding Tanya captive, and no claims were ever presented to the court.

Hose attempted suicide by stabbing himself in the stomach the day before the trial was to commence in February 2007. In March he received treatment for further mental issues and suicidal ideation, delaying the trial again.

Hose pleaded guilty to all charges in July 2007, avoiding a trial and a possible 100-year sentence.

In court, Jerry Kach stated he had spoken with Thomas Hose when Tanya was missing, and asked if he knew anything of Tanya's disappearance. Hose denied knowing of her whereabouts. Jerry Kach said in court, "I would have loved to see him get the death penalty for this."

Tanya stated in court that she never suffered any physical violence from Hose.

"I believe she was unhappy with her life and desperate with her situation and mustered the courage to come forward," said Kach's attorney, Lawrence Fisher. "Was it a particular event? I think it was a cumulative nature."

Thomas Hose was sentenced to five to 15 years in prison. Hose was denied parole in February 2012. His next parole date is in 2014.

Judith Sokol pleaded no contest to aiding and abetting statutory sexual assault, interference with the custody of a child, corruption of a minor, and child endangerment. She was sentenced to six to 23 months in jail with four years probation.

AFTERMATH

By September 2006, Kach launched numerous civil cases against people and organisations connected with the case. The courts rejected the litigation because the statute of limitations had passed.

In October 2011, Tanya Kach released *Memoir of a Milk Carton Kid*.

Jerry Kach and Tanya's former therapist, Janice Pope, launched litigation against Kach and Lawrence Fisher, co-author and former attorney, for defamation due to the contents of the book. Tanya's relationship with her father broke down soon after her escape. The book tells of her on-going conflict with Jerry Kach, and how she rejects him as her father. Jerry Kach didn't believe Tanya's claims that she was abducted and held captive.

"Some girls use what they got. This guy fell for it: hook, line, and sinker." Jerry Kach stated he wanted to hear Hose's side of the story, a comment that caused him to become estranged from his daughter.

Janice Pope provided Kach with free therapy sessions, but Kach claimed Pope "abandoned" her. Pope's attorney applied to seal the case from the public because it would expose confidential information disclosed by Kach.

When discussing the civil case, Lawrence Fisher told

Kach, " . . . if I've written something that is untrue, then it's your fault."

Janice Pope died in March 2013, before the civil case could proceed. She was 70.

Tanya owns a home, and lives with her partner and his children. She has remade contact with her mother. She has fallen out with a number of people related to the case. Tanya has suffered a number of health issues, which she contributes in part to being held by Hose, causing her to spend months in hospital and leaving her unable to have children.

Judith Sokol maintains her innocence, despite pleading no contest, considering herself betrayed by Kach. She claims she doesn't recall giving assistance to the desperate teen. She lost her apartment and her employment because of the ordeal.

Eleanor Hose died on February 7, 2103, aged 82. Tom Hose's son, Justin, now has a family of his own. There is speculation that he is writing a book about Tanya Kach and his father.

Kimberlie Krimm's murder remains unsolved.

Thomas Hose plans to tell his version of events once released from prison.

CHAPTER 16

NATASCHA KAMPUSCH

STRASSHOF, NIEDERÖSTERREICH – AUSTRIA.

2006

Birgitta Sirty (née Kampusch) was worried when her usually punctual daughter was ten minutes late. She contacted her school and discovered that Natasha did not attend that day. Her world ripped apart beneath her feet. Birgitta sat and watched the phone, hoping someone would call and inform her about Natascha's whereabouts. Eight years later the phone rang.

LEAD UP TO CRIME

World War II left its mark of terror on many people. When the Cold War later took its stranglehold on the world's consciousness, many people took preparatory measures, fearing the worst. Oskar Priklopil decided to construct a bomb shelter under his garage. In 1984, following his death, and that of his wife, his grandson Wolfgang Priklopil inherited the house and set about transforming the bomb shelter to possess a much more sinister purpose.

Wolfgang Priklopil, 35, was a self-employed telecommunications technician working for Siemens. He had a demanding personality, specifically when it came to females: slim, blonde, and well kept.

Priklopil lived alone in the large house, a shy man who never married. He had few friends, and those close to him never suspected there was anything malevolent behind his quiet façade. He was a man with an obsessive nature, resulting in compulsive cleaning.

Priklopil worked with close friend Ernest Holzapfel, renovating flats before placing them up for sale. During this time, Priklopil asked for Holzapfel's advice on how to soundproof a room, enough to hide the sound of a hammer drill. Priklopil used the techniques he learned while renovating flats to convert the bomb shelter into a dungeon. Priklopil lined the walls with mineral wool, a thick synthetic fibrous blanket, commonly used for thermal and acoustic insulation in structures or around pipes. In the bomb shelter, now hidden behind a safe and a concrete slab door, he fitted a bunk, toilet, and sinks. The process of venturing through the sealed doorways and into the dungeon took almost an hour.

On March 2, 1998, Priklopil made the 20 kilometre journey to Donaustadt, Vienna. Waiting in the street by his van, Priklopil spotted ten-year-old Natascha Kampusch walking to school, not far from where she lived with her single mother on an impoverished housing estate. He dragged her into his white van and drove her to his house in the upmarket satellite town of Strasshof. Priklopil took her inside the garage of 60 Heine Strasse, Strasshof, Lower Austria (Heine-Straße 60, 2231 Strasshof an der Nordbahn, Gänserndorf, Niederösterreich, Austria).

Priklopil moved aside the safe that covered the entrance and dragged Natascha down into the dank cell that crawled with insects. He locked her in the dark.

HELD CAPTIVE

Priklopil used physical torture to control Natascha, beating her more than 200 times a week. He also engaged in methods to remove her identity, by taking away her clothes and shaving her head.

"You're no longer Natascha. Now you belong to me," he instructed. He insisted that he be called "Master" and "My Lord."

Priklopil enjoyed the ritual humiliation and was

encouraged by Natascha's resistance. The painful beatings resulted in broken bones. Her body became so injured and bruised that she was unable to move. Priklopil would become enraged when Natascha cried, afraid the salt-acid of her tears would ruin the dungeon tiles. He held her under water or choked her until she passed out.

Wolfgang Priklopil's goal was to break Natascha Kampusch down until she became completely submissive. He restricted her food intake to keep her in a state of constant weakness, and forced her to clean his house. She spent long periods of time naked, even while completing her chores for her master.

When Natascha was 14, Priklopil removed her from the dungeon and chained her to himself, while they slept together in his bed. She would lie next to him, too frightened to move as he cuddled her. Soon their relationship begun to take on some elements of normality as a routine developed. They shared meals — Priklopil always portioned out Natascha's food — and as she spent more time above ground she was allowed to read and study from books in his library.

By the age of 16 Natascha weighed only 38 kilograms (84 pounds) and was 175 centimetres (5 foot 7 ½ inches) tall. She was forced to work and Priklopil mentally abused her to lower her feelings of self worth.

"The kidnapper knew precisely which buttons he had to push to land blows to my self esteem, and he pressed them mercilessly," said Natascha.

Priklopil would eventually allow her to accompany him into the backyard at night for short intervals, but the confinement was having drastic affects on Natascha and she attempted suicide on numerous occasions.

Police interviewed Priklopil in the days following Natascha's abduction, inspecting his van, before abandoning the lead. Neighbours would report him as a person they suspected of being involved in the kidnapping. Despite his name appearing several times, police would fail to partake in any meaningful investigation of Priklopil. Police did however follow the lead of a private investigator who was convinced Natascha's mother was having an affair with a local businessman, and together they murdered the girl and buried her in a pond on his property, in order for their relationship to continue.

As the years passed, Priklopil grew more confident and now believed Natascha stayed with him out of choice. They went for drives together, but he always held strict control over her. He made her carry heavy items to stop her from fleeing, and threatened he would kill any witnesses if she tried to escape. She had to always walk in front of him, staying within centimetres of him at all times. Despite being out in public, including on a skiing trip, Natascha did not have the opportunity to escape.

ESCAPE

"You have brought a situation upon us in which only one of us can make it through alive. I really am grateful to you for not killing me . . . This situation must come to an end," Natascha told Priklopil. She expected her comment to bring on a beating, which never came; all it brought was a forlorn look to her captor's face.

On Wednesday, August 26, 2006, Priklopil made Natascha vacuum his red BMW sports car. With the kidnap van parked in the backyard, he stood by and monitored Natascha, but a phone call broke his vigilance. While speaking on the phone, he stepped away from the sound of the vacuum. Natascha saw her opportunity to escape. Priklopil had left the gate open. She fled down the laneway and jumped a fence into a neighbouring yard. Through a kitchen window she saw an old woman and raised her attention, asking the woman to contact the police, stating her name was "Natascha Kampusch." The old woman told her to wait in the hedge, and not tread on the grass, while she called for the police.

Natascha had been held captive for 3,096 days, or eight-and-a-half years. She was now 18-years-old.

While Natascha finally made her escape, so did Priklopil. The now 44-year-old Priklopil was driven around Vienna for a few hours, confessing his crimes to his friend Ernest Holzapfel. Holzapfel let Priklopil out of the car near Wien Praterstern Railway Station, one of Vienna's main rail transportation hubs, 25 kilometres (15.5 miles) from his dungeon in Strasshof. Wolfgang Priklopil walked onto the train tracks, lay down, and a train ran over his head.

When Natascha heard of the suicide she burst into tears, inconsolable. She later visited Priklopil in the morgue, lighting a candle in his memory. He was buried in a secret location. Such was the national anger in Austria he was entombed under a different name to prevent his grave being desecrated.

AFTERMATH

Intense media attention surrounding the Natascha Kampusch case saw her shy away from interviews and from publically detailing many aspects of her captivity. For years Natascha refused to speak about whether she was sexually abused during her captivity, though police stated that such claims formed part of her initial complaint. She also considers the media invasion of her privacy another form of abuse, along with the constant speculation that she was used in a paedophilia ring, and she believes the media should be punished for their intrusion.

Surprisingly, Natascha didn't feel as though she had missed out on aspects of growing up, taking positives from her self-styled education.

Wolfgang's mother, Waltraud Priklopil, changed her name due to the large amount of public attention. She claimed to have no knowledge of the dungeon. She noticed around the time Wolfgang kidnapped Natascha that he became constantly nervous and withdrawn.

Natascha bought the house where she was held captive, keeping it sealed off from sightseers.

"It's my room, and not destined for the public to see," she stated to the media.

In 2010 she allowed a documentary crew into the house, where she spoke about her captive years, the house had been left virtually untouched since the day she fled. She believes Wolfgang Priklopil was either mentally ill, or desperately seeking to fill a void in his life in the only way he could imagine. She found the courage to forgive him.

Natascha hosted her own short-lived talk show. A movie based on Natascha Kampusch's book *3096 Days* was released in February 2013. Before the release of the movie she spoke publically that Priklopil repetitively raped her, and at the age of 25 she finally felt comfortable talking about it.

Natascha's career goal is to become a psychologist.

CHAPTER 17

KEVIN DAVIES

BREAM, GLOUCESTERSHIRE – ENGLAND.

2006

When a young boy kicked a football over a neighbour's garden fence, he could not have comprehended what was occurring on the other side. As he peered over to search for his ball, he was slammed with a barrage of swearing and screaming. He had no idea what secret his aggressive neighbours were protecting. On the other side, Kevin Davies was in desperate need of help that was unlikely to arrive.

LEAD UP TO CRIME

Kevin Davies, a 29-year-old epileptic handyman, moved into a house with Amanda Baggus, 26, a former care assistant, David Lehane, 36, and their nine-year-old son. The house is located on a well-kept estate on Badgers Way in the township of Bream, Gloucestershire, in southwest England, near the River Severn, with a population of just 2,600.

The Badgers Way house is positioned in a cul-de-sac, nestled along the winding roads that cut through the rolling hills in the Forest of Dean. Double story brick homes line the roads, all similar in style, not standing out from their neighbours. On long summer nights the local lads play football on the road, far from the dangers of traffic. The quiet hilltop setting awards views of a rich green valley and farmland. However, the idyllic country way of life was already deteriorating as unemployment, drugs, and daytime drinking took root throughout the English countryside.

Within the township of Bream, Baggus and Lehane were known for their wayward behaviour, "hillbillies" they were called, and many people avoided them.

Kevin Davies had previously moved to Bream from a nearby town after the council re-housed him, and having no friends he took to Baggus and Lehane. The trio began drinking together. Kevin worked at David Lehane's illegal backyard mechanic operation, and as a handyman who also cleaned the yards of the elderly.

Kevin's father died in March 2006. During this period, Baggus, and those in her company, were putting pressure on the intellectually impaired Davies in order to take advantage of his social security benefits.

Kevin announced to his mother that he was giving up his council flat — he was now technically homeless. She sensed at this time something was wrong, but she knew her son was a free spirit who would roam the country hills, and did not think she should intervene.

Due to his father's death just two months earlier, and encouraged by his new circle of friends, Kevin began drinking heavily. He needed a placed to stay. He was offered the shed down the side of the Badgers Way house.

The friendship then took a dangerous turn. When Baggus was driving her Reliant Robin three-wheeled vehicle, the car became unbalanced and suffered damage. Baggus blamed Davies, claiming he had opened the door too early, causing the car to overturn. Even though Davies had already handed over his benefits to Baggus and was working for Lehane, he was also expected to pay for the damage by working around the house.

From May 27, 2006, Kevin Davies was effectively taken as a slave.

HELD CAPTIVE

Kevin Davies was confined to a homemade shed, constructed from old building materials and positioned against a fence. Along with being forced to complete daily chores, Kevin had to endure extreme humiliation, daily beatings, and was treated like a dog. On one occasion, a cross was branded into Kevin's buttocks with a knife, on another occasion he was forced to drink weed killer.

Scott Andrews, 27, moved into the Badgers Way residence in July 2006. He became aware Kevin was being held captive in the shed. Rather than helping Kevin, Andrews participated in the attacks. He moved out of the house on September 7, 2006.

Amanda Baggus decided to keep a diary and video recordings of the events while Kevin was held in the garden shed for over four months. In her diary she recorded how he would plead for help, and described him with disdain as she detailed how he was tortured. The shocking video captured a weak and frightened Davies appearing in what can only be described as a "hostage-style video," with a black curtain used to block out distinguishing features of the house.

"And are you being fed nicely and everything?" a voice asks.

"I'm being fed perfectly, actually," stammers Davies. "I'm . . . I have been previously enjoying it. It's very good."

Kevin barely survived on potato peelings and kitchen

scraps. He appeared gaunt in the videos, his eyes sunken, and his head recently shaved. Kevin was threatened that he would be killed if he made any comments on the video that could identify his captors. He was forced to tell the camera he was a voluntary participant and agreed to how he was treated.

Baggus' diary revealed more of her sadistic nature.

Baggus' diary entry:

> *"21-07-06 Fri*
>
> Decided to make sure Kevin had a good night by getting Dave to beat him up."

Baggus' diary entry:

> *"5-08-06 Sat*
>
> he was playing up Late nite, banging in the shed. So Later that nite both Scott +Dave hit prick until quite late, cause prick made aload of shouting. Hoovered 3 times. Dave got back about 5ish, he seem in a good mood. Ang pick jovi up about 8ish."

To keep up appearances, Kevin was taken on an outing to the pub where his mother worked. She noticed he was thin, but thought it was because of his father's death. He assured her he was fine. He was then taken back to the tiny shed. Baggus and Lehane later allowed Kevin to call his mother and stepfather during his captivity, but only to reassure them that he was well.

Kevin's beatings became regular, often with a wooden club. Blood stained the walls and the ceiling of the shed, leaving a virtual blood-splatter map of his beatings. Kevin Davies finally died after Baggus bludgeoned him around the head with a plastic jug. Before she called for help she cleaned up the blood from his wounds.

DISCOVERY

On September 26, 2006, paramedics were called to Badgers Way, after receiving a report that Kevin Davies had suffered a seizure. Baggus told emergency workers Davies collapsed after he had walked 14 kilometres (nine miles) to her house.

Paramedics found Kevin's emaciated body on Baggus' kitchen floor. He suffered from malnourishment and torture. Along with cuts and scratches covering his body, Kevin had broken ribs and a broken larynx. One detective stated, "His body just gave up on him."

Forensics revealed Davies' body was covered in ten percent burns; a pathologist believed some were made with the heated blade of a knife. He had also been burnt with a corrosive liquid; and suffered bruising that covered his limbs, genitalia, and stretched across his jaw.

TRIAL

The accused were originally charged with murder, though those charges were later dropped, as Kevin's severe epilepsy was unable to be ruled out as a contributing factor causing his death. The trio were charged with unlawful killing, with Baggus and Lehane sentenced to serve ten years imprisonment. Scott Andrews was given nine years imprisonment.

Prosecutors told the court, "He had been assaulted, he had been beaten and he had effectively been kept like a dog in a locked garden shed at night. In short, the last few months of this man's life must have been utterly miserable and inhumane."

Davies' mother stated on conviction, "Although nothing can compensate us for Kevin's death, we feel the sentences validate our faith in British Justice." His mother also stated, "I just can't believe that anybody could be so cruel. I just still can't get my head round it. It just seems unreal. It gives you nightmares, it's on your mind 24/7 - it's just all the time thinking about him. I just don't know how they got away with it for so long."

Justice Gray, who presided over the case, stated, "His life was to have lacked structure. He needed sympathetic treatment, but what you meted out to him over many weeks was the very opposite of that."

In October 2010 Baggus was allowed out on day-release from prison to work in a charity shop as she prepares for her eventual release. She remains at H.M. Prison Send, near Woking, Surrey.

CHAPTER 18

DANIELLE CRAMER

WEST HARTFORD, CONNECTICUT

— UNITED STATES.

2007

Danielle Cramer was a teenage girl who loved animals and worked as a dog trainer. Within the leafy green suburbs of Connecticut, her life was slowly unravelling. She found a group of people who she thought would take her in, take care of her, but to them she was simply another stray without any protection, desperately looking for a safe place to call home.

LEAD UP TO CRIME

Adam Gault, 41, owned an animal training business. He sold the business to Jamie Hesse, and on occasion the pair worked together training dogs. Gault took an interest in Hesse's stepdaughter, Danielle Erica Cramer, 14.

As the pair became closer, Gault took Danielle under his wing, and helped her file a sexual abuse complaint with police shortly before her disappearance, after the teenager confided in Gault that she had been abused by a family friend. Police closed the complaint due to insufficient evidence.

"The missing girl did file a complaint with the Bloomfield Police Department over a year ago, claiming sexual and physical abuse in her own home. Nothing was done about it, and so she ran away," said Attorney Michael Georgetti.

Danielle was known to be a good student who came from a troubled upbringing and had a history of running away from home, having done so around five times previously. Police had labelled her current disappearance as a runaway, but under suspicious circumstances.

Danielle was a "...child from troubled circumstances and found what she believed to be a friend," according to Captain Jeffrey Blatter of the Bloomfield Police.

It is unclear if Danielle was being abused at home, but the abuse she was about to receive at the hand of Gault would be much worse.

Adam Gault shared a white aluminium-sided, double story house with his common law wife Ann Murphy, 40, and their 16-year-old son. They also shared the house with another woman, Gault's girlfriend, Kimberly Cray, 26.

Gault had a history of questionable involvement with female minors. In 1998, Gault was discovered to be hiding two 15-year-old runaway girls. One victim requested the court seal the arrest warrant application, concerned it may one day be used to identify her, which in tern hid aspects of Gault's previous actions from investigators.

HELD CAPTIVE

Danielle Cramer went missing from her home in Bloomfield, Connecticut, on June 14, 2006. It is unclear how she made it to Gault's house at 258 Newington Road, West Hartford, Connecticut, but once inside she was unable to leave.

Police believed the teenager had been murdered.

While held captive, Danielle was forced to appear in amateur porn, sex shows and modelling, which were uploaded to the internet. She was also forced to assume a new name and identity, to show that she was a part of the Gault "family," taking on the last name of Murphy. Any time she left the house with Gault she was presented as his niece. Danielle was taken out of the state at least one time.

Danielle's captors claimed she regularly attended school and she was free to come and go as she pleased, but police found no records indicating that Danielle attended any school. It is believed Danielle was intimidated into staying at the house.

In 2006, police were called after an argument between Gault and the landlord of a commercial premise he rented in Bloomfield. Inside the premises, police found bedding, a couch, video equipment and a tripod nearby, but took the matter no further. The landlord saw no evidence of sexual activity, but evicted Gault for housing and abusing animals on the premises.

RESCUE

Police interviewed Gault several times, suspecting him in connection with Danielle's disappearance, but he denied any involvement. Authorities looked into cell phone records, which indicated Gault and Danielle had talked on the phone several times before she went missing.

Danielle's parents released her diary to police; it indicated a sexual relationship with Adam Gault. Danielle stated that Gault had given her drugs and alcohol during the time she worked at his dog training business. She had begun a sexual relationship with Gault in November 2005, and stayed with him on two previous occasions when she had run away. Along with the diary, her family also turned over Danielle's seamen stained underwear, nine months after her disappearance. DNA linked the underwear to Gault.

Police believed Gault forced Danielle to undergo an abortion a month before her disappearance. While she would not claim who the father was, her foetus underwent forensic testing at a research clinic. Police approached Gault's home with a search warrant in the Danielle Cramer murder investigation, to obtain his DNA to prove that he was the father and possibly her killer.

Police had visited Gault multiple times in the investigation into Danielle's disappearance, but he was just one of several suspects on their radar.

On June 6, 2007, police attended the Newington Street address with a warrant, expecting to find Danielle's body. When police enacted their latest line of enquiry, the knock on the door went unanswered for several minutes.

As police searched the premises, one officer noticed a small door under a staircase, blocked by a large cabinet. Moving the cabinet, they discovered a crawlspace, about one-metre high by one-and-a-half metres deep (3 feet high x 5 feet deep), and also discovered the missing teenager. She had made no attempt to call for help as police searched the house.

Once found, she emerged in tears, wearing only a shirt and shorts. The lack of bedding indicated she did not live in the crawlspace, but it was rather used as a way to avoid police detection. Danielle was very pale from lack of sunlight, but did not show any signs of physical abuse. She was also in a confused state and could not remember her name. It's believed Danielle had been inside the house on all earlier occasions when police attended and was she being hidden when they knocked on the door.

Danielle was reunited with her mother a few days later, but only for a couple of hours, before returning to protective custody in a psychiatric hospital to receive months of therapy.

Gault was arrested and charged with unlawful restraint, interfering with an officer, second-degree forgery, reckless endangerment and custodial interference. His bond was initially set at $1 million, but as additional charges were added, his bail would rise to $2.35 million. Murphy and Cray were arrested and charged with conspiracy and risk of injury. Murphy's bond would total $950,000, while Cray's would reach $750,000.

Police also found a collection of low-quality, blurry homemade porn tapes at Gault's residence. Investigations attempted to identify several other girls on the tapes, in cases that stretched across several states and involved the FBI.

Danielle's case inspired three other girls to come forward. All had similar experiences, stating that Gault "uses fear and intimidation to control people."

Adam "had a history of taking stray people in," according to Gault's friend Jeff Cornfield.

TRIAL

The kidnappers of Danielle Cramer claimed they were offering her a safe haven to hide. Police were sceptical and described the residence as filthy and unkempt, with rooms filled with trash and debris, while the whole house had a foul odour.

Police observed that Adam Gault had a history of grooming female minors, targeting those who had low self-esteem, family problems and troubled home lives. Gault would control these girls by giving them drugs, alcohol, employment and a certain amount of attention. He has been tied to other cases of a similar nature.

Adam Gault was arraigned in August 2007 in relation to the Danielle Cramer case. He was charged with first degree kidnapping, first degree conspiracy to commit kidnapping, second degree sexual assault, risk of injury to a minor, conspiracy to commit risk of injury, and conspiracy to impair the morals of a minor. At one point in his trial, Gault claimed he was too mentally incompetent to stand, but experts quickly dismissed his claim.

After the hearing, Kimberly Cray's attorney, Michael Georgetti, said: "The girl was never molested in that house. There are no allegations of molestation."

The defence attorney claimed his clients were only holding the girl to protect her from her abusive parents.

The plaintiff attorney responded, "So these people were saving her from abusive parents and exploiting her to do porn on the internet? Isn't that rich."

The attorney for Danielle Cramer's parent's, Marc Needelman, rejected the claim as "a total fabrication" that she was abused at the family home. He went on to say, "The Bloomfield police department had been involved in the investigation over a year. They publicly stated yesterday in no uncertain terms that the girl's parents have absolutely no responsibility, have committed no crimes or engaged in any improprieties."

AFTERMATH

Danielle's parents filed a civil suit against Gault, Murphy and Cray. They requested to freeze the trios assets up to $1 million and be awarded an additional $15,000 in damages. The suit stated that Danielle suffered from false imprisonment, intentional infliction of emotional distress, battery and assault. Her kidnapper's actions had caused her long-term emotional trauma, mental pain and anguish, and embarrassment and humiliation. Her parents also included their own emotional turmoil in the suit.

Adam Gault received a 50-year prison sentence, suspended after 25 years, which included a five-year sentence for a charge of kidnapping another girl in 1998, who came forward when she heard of Gault's arrest in the Danielle Cramer case. Gault was not charged with sexual assault for this other woman because the time limit for prosecution had expired. His sentence will be followed by

20 years probation.

Ann Murphy and Kimberly Cray were both sentenced to three years in prison. The Gault's son was placed in state care.

Danielle Cramer's parents, Jamie and Jennifer Hesse, appeared on *Larry King Live* where they spoke with Ed Smart, father of Elizabeth Smart, about Danielle's ordeal.

CHAPTER 19

ELISABETH FRITZL

AMSTETTEN, NIEDERÖSTERREICH – AUSTRIA.

2008

In 2008, the world paused in horror as the news broke. A man in Austria was discovered to have kept an incestuous family in a dungeon beneath his home. The Fritzl case would be one of the worst cases of abuse the world had ever witnessed, and become the most famous instance of humans held captive.

LEAD UP TO CRIME

Josef Fritzl grew up in poverty. His father constantly cheated on his mother, and she threw him out of the house when Josef was four-years-old, thereafter raising the boy on her own. She only gave birth to the child to prove to her husband that she was not infertile. Josef grew up in the Nazi era where ruling parties demanded strictness, as did his mother, who ignored him except when she often beat him. He attended school in Amstetten, two years older than his classmates, he proved to be highly intelligent.

As a teenager Fritzl would indulge in sexual fantasies about his mother, and considered himself her husband. He met Rosemarie in 1956, and married her a year later.

As Rosemarie gave birth to their first child in 1957, Fritzl rode his bike around town, peering in people's windows, but claimed he was working late at the steel factory to support his family.

Elisabeth was born on April 6, 1966; she was the fourth of seven children. She was a painfully shy child, timid to approach adults. Fritzl often beat his daughter, and Rosemarie claimed he didn't like Elisabeth.

On October 6, 1967, he was arrested for raping a woman in her apartment at knifepoint in Linz, and served 12 months of an 18-month sentence. He had also committed other attacks on local women. When released from prison, Rosemarie forgave him.

In 1973, having established himself as a successful

businessman, Fritzl bought the Seesteern Guesthouse at Mondsee, in the lakes district of Upper Austria. During this time he imprisoned his elderly mother in the attic of the family home, until she died in 1980.

Fritzl began sexually abusing Elisabeth at the age of 11. In 1981/82 (when Elisabeth was around 15 years old) Fritzl began making plans for the cellar beneath their family home at Ybbstrasse Number 40, Amstetten, Lower Austria. He planned to transform it into a homemade prison.

The guesthouse was destroyed by fire in 1982. Police arrested Fritzl on suspicion of arson and held him for 14 days, but the charges were dropped due to insufficient evidence. Fritzl collected the insurance money.

As Elisabeth matured, she became more assertive, much to her father's displeasure. In 1983 she ran away from home with a friend, fleeing to Vienna. The pair was caught by police after three weeks and returned to Josef Fritzl.

In the same year, planning permits were approved for Fritzl to commence additional work on his cellar, and he enlisted the help of his brother-in-law to carry out the works. He had very specific plans; including that the ceiling should be only 1.7 metres (5.5 feet) high. Only Fritzl himself knew the true purpose of his plans.

HELD CAPTIVE

On August 28, 1984, when Elisabeth was 18, Fritzl lured her downstairs by asking her to help carry the door that would seal the dungeon. He drugged her with ether, and held her captive. Fritzl chained his daughter to a wall, unlocking her only to rape her. He wrote fake letters, claiming Elisabeth had joined a cult. Cults had gained a negative reputation during the seventies and eighties, with mass media portraying them as groups that isolated and brainwashed their members. Fritzl's story seemed plausible, especially when it came to the troublesome and wayward girl Fritzl made his daughter out to be.

Fritzl warned Elisabeth that if anyone touched the cellar door they would be electrocuted. Inside the cell, measuring four-and-a-half metres squared (15 x 15 feet), was Elisabeth's world for nine years. Josef Fritzl visited the dungeon every few days, using a remote control to open the heavy door, providing supplies and raping his daughter. She was raped over 3,000 times, violently inserting her with objects that caused permanent physical injuries, and forced her to re-enact scenes from pornographic films.

Fritzl was suspected of the unsolved murder of Martina Posch, 17, who was found wrapped in plastic near the guesthouse in 1986. He continued running the guesthouse until 1996.

Elisabeth gave birth in isolation to seven children.

Kerstin was born in 1988. Three unfortunate children — Kerstin, the eldest, Stefan and Felix — grew up in the dungeon.

On April 28, 1996, Elisabeth gave birth to twin boys, Michael and Alexander. Michael died three days later, Fritzl cremated his body in the furnace and scattered his ashes throughout the garden.

Three children — Lisa, Monika and Alexander — would live seemingly normal lives upstairs. Everyone was led to believe Elisabeth, unable to care for her children while she lived her cultish lifestyle, had dropped them off on the doorstep in the dark of night.

As Fritzl's underground family grew, so did the dungeon as he covertly constructed additional rooms. The small confines of the cell were filled with stale air, leaving the captives listless, barely able to move. A rancid, sick smell engulfed the cavern. Condensation dripped from the tiled walls. The two-bedroom dungeon was soundproofed and included a bathroom, toilet, and kitchen. The lack of natural light would leave the children weak, sickly, and pale. The moisture provided a perfect environment for mould to grow, causing fungal infections for the captives. They suffered malnutrition, vitamin D deficiencies, and severe dental problems. Stefan suffered from motor neurone problems. The children's only understanding of the outside world came from what they watched on an old television, and from what their mother taught them.

In 1998 Fritzl went on a four-week holiday to Thailand, leaving Elisabeth and her three children behind in the cellar. He bought her dresses, claiming they were for his girlfriend. Rosemarie was unaware of the secret family her husband hid beneath her feet.

RESCUE

Kerstin, now 19, became desperately ill, suffering from uncontrollable screaming fits and lapsing into unconsciousness. On April 19, 2008, she was taken to hospital by ambulance, along with a letter Fritzl made Elisabeth write, begging the hospital to take care of her daughter. With no medical records or personal documentation, the hospital became suspicious of Kerstin's identity.

The young woman presented to doctors was suffering from multiple organ failure and placed in an induced coma as doctors worked to help her recover. Doctors made a public appeal over Austrian television on April 21, asking for Elisabeth to contact authorities. Elisabeth watched the story ignite, and begged her father to take her to the hospital.

On April 26, Fritzl decided to release his captive family from their underground prison. Elisabeth, Stefan, and Felix made their way upstairs, where Fritzl told Rosemarie their prodigal daughter had returned home. Elisabeth Fritzl had been missing for 8,516 days. After nearly 24 years she was finally free.

Once in the hospital grounds, Josef and Elisabeth were detained. Elisabeth refused to provide information on her circumstance until she was promised she would never have to see her father again. In the early hours of the morning, on April 27, 2008, Josef Fritzl was arrested. By nightfall, Rosemarie and all the children were taken into state care.

TRIAL

Three hundred officers initially worked on the Fritzl case. On March 16, 2009, the trial against Austria's incest dungeon master began.

Josef Fritzl, 73, pleaded guilty to false imprisonment, incest, and rape; but pleaded not guilty to enslavement and murder by neglect.

Elisabeth testified via an 11-hour pre-recorded video presented to the court. Josef Fritzl sat in the courtroom in St Pölten and listened to his daughter's testimony. Neither Rosemarie nor Elisabeth's children testified. Jurors found the case especially difficult, and extra jurors were kept on standby in case any original jurors could not continue.

During the four-day trial, Elisabeth dressed in a wig and entered the courtroom to watch the proceedings. Her father turned around and saw her. He began to weep.

After watching Elisabeth's testimony, Fritzl changed his plea to "guilty" on all charges. On March 19, 2009, he was sentenced to life imprisonment, to be detained in a psychiatric hospital.

Fritzl must serve 15 years before he is first eligible for parole in 2024. He will be 89 years old. He is currently held in a secure ward for the criminally insane at Garsten Abbey in Upper Austria; a former Benedictine abbey, with a near millennia long history, converted to a high security prison. He is prisoner number 4546765. Fritzl is permanently isolated because of his risk of being attacked by other prisoners. He suffers from dementia.

AFTERMATH

Elisabeth Fritzl and her basement children spent months in a secure psychiatric hospital while they recovered from their torturous ordeal. Elisabeth had aged far beyond her years. She attempted to re-establish a relationship with her mother, but her anger boiled over when she questioned why Rosemarie never tried to help. Elisabeth threw her mother out of their villa nestled in the grounds of the psychiatric hospital.

The captives took on new names, and were moved to a secure location only known as "Village X," a short distance from Amstetten. Security personnel and CCTV guard her home. Local villagers are only too willing to contact police if sightseers are spotted.

The upstairs and downstairs family has reunited, and all have undergone psychological therapy and schooling. Elisabeth decided to discontinue with psychiatric care. She now understands that her mother was also a victim and the pair has mended their relationship. Rosemarie lives in a small flat in Linz, sells homemade bags to supplement her pension, and visits her family each week.

After their release, Elisabeth would shower several times a day, and became compulsive about cleaning. Closed doors distressed the children, and doors were fixed to remain open or removed from the hinges altogether. Treatment is expected to be on going with all the children.

Elisabeth has worked to gain her drivers licence. Despite her shying away from media attention, paparazzi have photographed her shopping, something which she enjoys doing. She was reported to have fallen in love with Thomas Wagner, a bodyguard 14 years her junior. A fulltime carer resides at their house, looking after Elisabeth and the children, especially when moments of panic overwhelm them.

Josef Fritzl wrote a series of letters to Elisabeth, requesting she send him money so he could defend himself by studying law. She no longer accepts his communications. In 2012, he divorced Rosemarie because she never visited him in prison.

As a means of reaching out, fellow Austrian and former captive, Natascha Kampusch, gave Elisabeth Fritzl 25,000 euros from funds publically donated to assist kidnap victims.

CHAPTER 20

MARIA MONACO

SANTA MARIA CAPUA VETERE, CASERTA

- ITALY.

2008

In a small Italian town, the Monaco family hid their stigma and shame away in a forgotten room of the house. For nearly two decades their secret was confined. The case rocked Italy, but was largely ignored and forgotten in the worldwide media frenzy surrounding the Fritzl case, which came to public attention just two months earlier.

LEAD UP TO CRIME

The picture postcard setting of Santa Maria Capua Vetere — a small medieval town in Southern Italy, known for its Roman ruins and its tourism — was home to a dark tale, in contrast to its picturesque surroundings. The sunny and slow paced town, about 40 kilometres north of Naples, was not the place many would expect to find a family who held captive one of their own.

In 1990, 29-year-old Maria Monaco did something that millions of women around the world do — she had a child out of wedlock. However, unlike families of other women, Maria's family did not provide her with a support structure; instead they became angry and consumed with shame. They forced Maria into her bedroom and locked her in there, a place they intended to hold her for the rest of her life.

The people directly responsible for holding her captive were those closest to her: Maria's mother, Anna Rosa Golino, 80, who ruled the family with an iron fist, but to the outside world looked like any kindly, rural Italian woman; her sister, Michelina Monaco, 54, who worked as a kindergarten teacher; and her brother, Prisco Monaco, 44, who worked as a farmer like his father, who died in 1985, five years before Maria was imprisoned.

The Monaco's held a good reputation with the locals, maintaining a positive outward appearance.

"Good people, one of the best families of St. Andrew,"

one local told a newspaper. The locals also knew of Maria, although that had not seen her in nearly twenty years.

From the outside, the entrance to the Monaco's two-story house doesn't stand out from its surroundings. It is along Via Cormons, a small winding alley, laid with asphalt and lined with ancient stone walls, leading to the town square. Heavy green iron gates protect the collection of houses within. The suburb, littered with centuries old buildings, backs onto farmland.

When Maria was in the early stages of her pregnancy, she received care from a health worker. But when the worker suddenly died a few months into the pregnancy, all health care for Maria ceased.

HELD CAPTIVE

On the balcony of the Monaco's house, white sheets air in the summer sun. From behind the doors facing a courtyard, the rank smell of urine seeps out. A passageway strewn with wet and dirty linen lines the way to Maria's room.

Maria's son was born in December 1990, from an undisclosed affair, after she had already spent much of her pregnancy locked away. He survived by being taken in by the family, where he lived with his grandmother, and was aware that his own mother was held in the family home. He was restricted from seeing his mother, being told she was too ill for visitors.

Maria Monaco was locked in her bedroom on the second floor; the room would not be cleaned for years. The filth and sheer inhumanity of Maria's prison shocked even the hard bitten police officers who rescued her from her decades long hell. Soiled mattresses and sheets, and the rancid stench of years of squalor hit them like a wave when they entered the room. The Spartan room contained grime encrusted furniture and a toilet caked with faeces. Mountains of cigarette butts surrounded the woman.

The room housed two battered beds, one with clean linen, the other soiled with blood and a large amount of faeces. Presumably, this allowed Maria to rotate between beds when they became filthy when covered in bodily fluids. Maria ate from dog bowls, drank from plastic water bottles, and used a chair for a table. The toilet had not worked for years, leaving Maria's excretion to cake around the room.

As much as the family had kept Maria's captivity a secret, some locals knew of her situation. The local church priest attended the house in 2002 to check on her care, but was turned away. A doctor had also been prescribing Maria medication. The family doctor was aware Maria was receiving medication, even though he never saw Maria or entered the house. The medication was collected by Michelina Monaco.

RESCUE

A report to police came from a neighbour who could no longer stand the stench coming from the Monaco house, believing someone was locked inside. Police made their way to the house on the edge of town to investigate.

When Italian police raided Anna Rosa Golino's home they were horrified by what they found. Maria was dazed and disoriented, brought on in all likelihood by years of torture and segregation from human contact. She cowered in a corner.

When Captain Carmine Rosciano entered, he stated, Maria "greeted us with a sound like a howl, a shriek inhuman."

Around lunchtime on June 13, 2008, Maria Monaco, now 47, was removed from her home-style prison, after being held captive for 18 years. On a makeshift stretcher she was led through the courtyard to an awaiting ambulance. Her face was swollen and puffy, covered with tangles of thick hair. A blue-green shirt covered her twisted and frail body.

Maria was taken to a hospital in Naples where she was treated for trauma, and later transferred to the psychiatric ward.

Lawyers for the family claimed the incarceration was for Maria's own good; claiming she had mental illness issues, and refused treatment. Instead of making use of available channels to force Maria into treatment, her family simply locked her away in silence and squalor for years, hiding all evidence of her existence from the outside world.

Officers reported that Maria was unable to walk properly, and that instead of speaking, she emitted an animal like wailing sound. In Italy, more so in rural areas, families often keep mentally ill or disabled members confined to the house.

All the family members were arrested and taken in for questioning. Michelina Monaco asked to fix her appearance, and change into her best dress and put on earrings, when asked to accompany the police to the station.

TRIAL

"This is a particularly horrible case," said prosecutor Antonio Ricci. "But this measure is often taken with the mentally ill, also because there is little access to health care in the most isolated areas."

Maria's original condition was certified after she gave birth, though the doctor who diagnosed her has not been discovered. Certification allowed the Monaco's to collect a disability pension on behalf of Maria, and an attendance allowance for themselves.

The lawyer for the family, Gianfranco Carbone, said: "The family was only trying to be discreet." He stated she was free to leave at any time, but Maria "has serious psychological problems and refused to undergo any therapy."

"What's happened is a drama within a drama," said Carbone.

Maria was a normal girl according to locals, who had heard "that after a disappointment in love" Maria was not well. Prosecutor Antonio Ricci supported the hypothesis that Maria was segregated to hide her pregnancy and the family shame at all costs, and the mental illness was a result caused or aggravated by the captivity.

Locals didn't remember a girl who was mentally ill two decades ago. "Never been sick, was not crazy." Only after she became pregnant did she vanish from everyone's sight. The locals had no idea who the 17-year-old boy's father might be.

Maria's son attended a local high school, and was known for being a "superior" student. Police and investigators handling the case were unable to ascertain who was the man that Maria had her affair with, and fathered her child.

The family members were charged with kidnapping and aggravated harassment. How they spent the money they received from the disability pension and attendance allowance was not evident. A family member stated it "went all in cigarettes [for Maria], we have not taken anything." They claimed she smoked around three to four packets a day.

AFTERMATH

Italian courts run on a mixture of their former inquisitional system and the more recently adopted adversarial system. The magistrate is a civil servant and may deliver justice swiftly.

Anna Rosa Golino was released from jail and placed under house arrest, due to her advanced age. The court ordered that she remain locked in the same house she held her daughter. Michelina and Prisco Monaco were both sentenced to prison in Santa Maria Capua Vetere.

Two months after he was imprisoned, Prisco Monaco was transferred to an infirmary because of illness. After his illness, he had to be rehoused in another location as other prisoners refused to share a cell with him. It is unclear how long both siblings stayed in prison, but as of early 2013 Prisco Monaco was registered at his Via Cormons address.

Maria received help at a psychiatric hospital in Naples and was placed in a reception home. She is unlikely to ever recover. Her son was sent to live with an uncle in a nearby town and studied to become a builder.

CHAPTER 21

KYLE RAMIREZ

TRACY, CALIFORNIA – UNITED STATES.

2008

Witnesses watched as an almost naked boy dropped over a fence and stumbled through the car park. Covered in an array of wounds and injuries, the gaunt boy carried a chain, still locked around his ankle. Not turning back, he could sense his captors weren't too far behind.

LEAD UP TO CRIME

Susan Barnett had three children: Brandon Cardiff, Austin Louisgnont, and Kyle Ramirez. Caren Ramirez was a friend of Barnett's, and Kyle considered her an aunt, though they were not related. The two youngest boys started living with Ramirez when Kyle was eight years old, after being removed from the custody of their abusive father. Barnett had scant involvement in her children's lives.

On September 20, 2005, Caren Ramirez sent her adopted son, Austin, 16, out onto the streets to panhandle. After spending the day begging around Citrus Heights, Sacramento, the boy returned home in the evening, sat on the couch, and revealed he had made only $9.00. News of the meagre takings sent Caren Ramirez into a violent rage.

Deputies from the Sacramento Sherriff's Department were dispatched to Caren Ramirez's home, responding to an assault in progress — a juvenile being hit by an adult. Police found Ramirez had forced Austin into her bedroom.

"I'm going to fuck you up," said Ramirez. "I heard you talking shit, saying that I'm not your mom!"

She beat him with a martial arts stick. As Austin attempted to cover his head, Ramirez screamed, "Don't put your hands up."

The woman told police Austin's injuries were sustained while he was play fighting with a friend. She stated Austin made the complaint against her after she took away his Game Boy, and that he had not taken his Ritalin in two months. Austin was removed and placed with a foster family.

In the early hours of the morning on May 30, 2006, police returned to the home of Caren Ramirez. Ramirez's biological daughter, Cristina Sanchez, 21, reported Kyle, 13, had shown her injuries garnered from his adopted aunt: bruised arms, legs, and buttocks, and a split and swollen lip. Caren Ramirez had beaten Kyle with a martial arts stick the day before the report was made. The boy revealed to police officers that when Ramirez was angry she also assaulted him with broom handles, a spatula, and a coat hanger.

Child Protective Services were called and Kyle was taken out of Caren Ramirez's care, and delivered to the Children's Receiving Home in Sacramento. His brother Austin, now 18, had been moved to foster care in Central California and had concerns about Kyle. Caren Ramirez stated the allegations made against her were inaccurate, but could not state what the inaccuracies were. She suffered from depression and anxiety and was prescribed Zoloft.

On May 9, 2007, Kyle was reported as a runaway from the receiving home — afraid of being placed in foster care.

Kyle had met with Caren Ramirez who convinced him to travel with her, first stopping at Pleasanton, California. They spent the summer living with Catherine Cockrell and her three children. She considered Kyle "lazy," who pillaged neighbours houses for food. Cockrell's son begged for his mother to kick the pair out, accusing Kyle of hogging the computer games.

The pair moved on to Tracy, California, and lodged with husband and wife, Michael Luther Schumacher and Kelly Layne Lau, and their four children.

Care workers from the receiving home failed to make contact with Cristina Sanchez through monthly phone calls.

On August 22, 2007, social worker, Linda Hirsch, was assigned Kyle's case, and discovered Caren Ramirez had been collecting his Social Security check, but the Social Security office refused to provide her with Ramirez's address. Police were not able to locate the boy. Hirsch made monthly attempts to locate Kyle, but her searches proved fruitless.

Sacramento County Department of Social Services reported Kyle Ramirez missing on March 27, 2008.

HELD CAPTIVE

Michael Schumacher, a contractor, and his wife, Kelly Lau, a Girl Scout leader, lived in a detached two-story home at 630 Tennis Lane, in the centre of Tracy, Sacramento. Their street was family friendly; where neighbours hung American flags from their porches and kept their lawns tidy. They had four children between the ages of one and nine, and often babysat the neighbours' children. They were friends of Catherine Corkrell. Caren and Kyle came to live in their house in July 2007.

Kyle was padlocked by his ankle and chained to a coffee table or the fireplace grill. They called the boy "Iggit" slang for *idiot*. He was forced to complete all the household chores, look after the infants, and kneel on the floor for hours. Kyle would also help the Schumacher children with their homework.

Neighbour Anthony Waiters, former youth football coach, assisted the adults of the Tennis Lane house in their torture of the boy. Waiters poured lighter fluid on Kyle and set his pants alight. Candlewax and superglue were used to patch Kyle's head wounds. A belt was used to strangle the boy until he blacked out. While unconscious his arm fell onto the fireplace grill and he suffered third-degree burns.

Kyle was also made to sleep in a wood-burning fireplace. An aluminium baseball bat was kept near the fireplace, heated in the flames, before Caren and Kelly would beat and brand him with it. The four adults took turns beating him on a daily basis with razors, mallets, belts and hammers. He has been left with permanent scars around his wrists, caused by being restrained with zip-ties. Michael Schumacher asked Lau for a syringe to pump air into the boy's veins.

When Kyle was sprayed with lighter fluid and set alight, "They were all just laughing at me because I was trying to put the fire out," said Kyle.

"They cut my arm and poured bleach on it. It burned," Kyle told the grand jury. "And then they tape it after — oh, my bad — they put butter and salt after they poured the bleach on."

Despite collecting Kyle's benefits, the household was suffering further financial trouble, and the electricity was cut off the month before his escape. The family used the fireplace to keep warm, with Kyle still shackled to it, causing him third-degree burns, as he couldn't escape.

A neighbouring girl played with Kyle noticed that he had lost "a lot" of weight. Kyle ate old Halloween candy and stale bread. He was forced to drink liquor provided to him and chew on marijuana, so he would never have the strength to fight back. The boy had been systematically tortured for over a year, and one way or another, his time was about to end.

ESCAPE

Kyle, now 16, heard Waiters and the Schumacher's planning to "chop me up and throw me in the Delta."

Kyle waited until his captors were distracted. He convinced Kelly and Michael's two-year-old son to get a set of keys left lying around the house. He unlocked his shackles. Bleeding and weak from starvation, Kyle managed to run out the backdoor. In the backyard he jumped on a trampoline, launched himself off a wall, and fell into a car park.

Around 4 p.m. on December 1, 2008, the emaciated boy burst into In-shape Sport, a fitness club, carrying a chain attached to his ankle. The event was recorded on CCTV. Kyle wore only a pair of boxer shorts, stained with urine and faeces. His body was covered in soot, bruises, burns, cuts, and scars.

"Hide me, please hide me. They're coming for me," begged the boy.

Shocked employees of the fitness club — initially thinking they were the recipients of a prank — let the boy hide behind the counter and wrapped him in towels, showing him the first ounce of human compassion he had seen in months. Employees called the police, while customers continued to approach the counter for service.

Kyle was taken to the Sutter Tray Community Hospital. In a grand jury statement, Linda Hirsch said, "He was very thin, fragile — he had burns, bruises on him." He spent 20 days recovering in a burns centre, where he received skin grafts for untreated third-degree burns. The burns would have restricted his movement if left to heal naturally.

Neighbours claimed that they did not think that there was anything suspicious going on in the Schumacher home, but some did see Kyle looking malnourished and weak. They however stated that it was not any of their business.

Schumacher and Lau were quickly arrested after Kyle's escape. Caren Ramirez was arrested soon afterwards, at an acquaintance's house. Anthony Waiters was arrested on December 9, 2008, in Pleasanton, where he worked in technical support for a realtor. They were held on $2.2 million bail.

TRIAL

All four of the accused were charged with torture, kidnapping, false imprisonment by violence, corporal injury to a child, child abuse, and aggravated mayhem.

Before the trial was set to proceed, three of the accused entered a plea bargain. Even though the case had become known as the "Tracy torture trial," the charge of torture was dropped.

On January 20, 2011, Michael Schumacher was sentenced to 30 years, and Kelly Lau was given 33 years in prison. Kelly Lau claimed she abused Kyle out of fear that Caren Ramirez would harm her own children.

Caren Ramirez was sentenced to 34 years behind bars. They must complete 85 percent of their sentences before they can apply for parole.

Anthony Waiters pleaded not guilty. Kyle testified against Waiters.

On November 23, 2010, Anthony Waiters was convicted for torturing, kidnapping, abusing and falsely imprisoning Kyle. In February 2011 he was sentenced to serve three consecutive life-terms, and denied parole for a period of 19 years. As the verdict was handed down,

Waiters still maintained his innocence.

AFTERMATH

Susan Barnett, Kyle's mother, died of cancer in 2008.

Kyle Ramirez and the Schumacher's four children were taken into protective custody. Kyle was later taken into the legal custody of his biological aunt and uncle, Sydney and Ralph Perry. Kyle took up playing football, returned to playing video games, and attended school. Litigation was brought against Sacramento Child Protective Services in February 2011, for their failure in taking action during the several years while Kyle was being abused, before he was held captive.

The large public outpouring for Kyle's plight saw $33,000 donated, to aid him on his road to recovery and towards a new life.

CHAPTER 22

LUCIA MONGELLI

TURIN, PIEDMONT — ITALY.

2009

Lucia Mongelli's family confined her for nearly 25 years. Her father subdued the female members of the Mongelli family through a "psychological reign of terror," and orchestrated the captivity by basing his beliefs on an archaic law, to feed his incestuous desires. Michele Mongelli would become known as the "Ogre of Falchera."

LEAD UP TO CRIME

Michele Mongelli, 64, lived in a small apartment in the downtrodden suburb of Falchera, on the outskirts of Turin, Italy. He lived with his family in a housing development area; an area stocked with plain housing blocks, surrounded by parklands lined with Cyprus trees and freeways. Michele and his wife Caterina had ten children, of which Lucia (also known in the press as "Laura") was the eldest daughter. Michele had been able to afford the apartment after receiving compensation for a car accident.

Michele worked with his eldest son, Giuseppe, 40, as a street vendor, driving around in a beat-up utility vehicle, collecting scrap metal from the streets of Turin to sell at markets. Over the years Michele and Giuseppe had had numerous dealings with police and social workers. Both had been arrested for theft. Social workers often checked on Carmine, the youngest Mongelli son, who was deaf.

Their rough exteriors were nothing compared to the brutality they were hiding within. Michele controlled his family to suit his incestuous nature, passing his abusive traits on to Giuseppe.

Michele had been enacting a medieval right known as *droit de seigneur* — a law of dubious nature — which allows the "right of the lord" of an estate to claim the virginity of any of his serfs' unwed daughters. Michele interpreted this to mean he was entitled to have sex with his daughters, telling them this was the usual custom.

"I am going to teach you a game before I touch you, which you will use when you are older," Michele Mongelli told Lucia, as the abuse started when she was aged nine.

HELD CAPTIVE

Lucia Mongelli's family removed her from school around 1988, when she was just 13, leaving her with a limited education. She was often confined to a darkened room with no electricity, received no further education, and had extremely limited contact with the outside world.

In 1994, Lucia escaped and contacted police, lodging a report. Michele pressured Lucia to blame her uncle, who denied the accusations. Her father managed to convince authorities that Lucia was mentally disturbed. All investigations ceased. The family received help from a psychologist, who failed to detect the abuse. It would be another sixteen years before the true issue came to light.

"From when I was aged nine my father forced me to suffer sexual acts, touching my private parts, kissing me on the mouth, and from age sixteen onwards forcing me to have full sexual intercourse with him," said Lucia.

Michele trained his son how to rape. Lucia was first raped at 16 by her brother Giuseppe, then by her father. Lucia was locked up, and the two family members repeatedly raped her over the following two weeks. She was later taken to hospital where she was forced to undergo an abortion. Michele ordered Lucia to tell doctors that she been "raped by a Moroccan."

One of Lucia's sisters would give birth: a child born of her own father.

News of the incest and captivity spread throughout their local community, causing the parish priest to ask Michele Mongelli questions. The priest was told to mind his own business. He did.

Over the years, Lucia was kept as a sex slave. She was allowed out of her room when accompanying her family on trips, where Giuseppe was placed in charge of watching her.

The abuse extended further into the family, with Giuseppe following in his father's footsteps and raping his own daughters. His four daughters, aged between six and 20, were also forced to watch him in sexual acts. It is also believed Michele Mongelli abused other members of his extended family.

Police would eventually receive a tip that would lead to Lucia's release.

RELEASE

A small toy horse peered from the shuttered window, looking out to the grassy parkland below, a tragic symbol of what was occurring inside. On the balcony, children's clothes hung from a line, and bed sheets from the railing.

A large collection of crucifixes, and photographs of St. Padre Pio — known as the priest with the stigmata, canonised in 2006 — hung on the white walls of the apartment. Of all the family photographs, only one image contained Lucia. She looked out from the frame, carrying a forlorn expression and dead eyes, her face bordered by a short haircut.

Police bugged the home phones and cars of Michele and Giuseppe Mongelli, after an unknown informant alerted them to the incest. The phone taps were installed incorrectly; accidently picking up audio from inside the apartment while the phone was not in use. Police recorded Giuseppe making inappropriate sexual advances to his eight-year-old daughter.

The tape captured the young girl saying, "Dad, get your hands off me. You are a bastard, stop it."

Giuseppe Mongelli was arrested on the February 23, 2009.

Lucia initially told police Giuseppe had raped her, but the investigation soon turned to her father, who they believed was the mastermind behind the plan.

Michele's voice was also recorded on tape saying, "Come on, you are mine. Get up." The sounds of sex followed.

Before police could take Michele into custody, he drove Lucia to an abandoned cottage near a local cemetery, where he forced her to perform oral sex on him one final time.

Police arrested Michele on March 28, 2009, freeing

Lucia from her father's abusive clutches after 25 years. She was now 34 years old.

TRIAL

The lawyer defending Michele Mongelli since his arrest stated his client was impotent because of diabetes, therefore he was unable to rape. His family also reiterated this, claiming he could not commit such crimes because of injuries sustained in a car accident.

Michele and Giuseppe were accused of rape, sexual assault, and obscene acts in public. Prosecutors said the two men ruled the family with a "psychological reign of terror."

"My husband goes around to metal markets," Caterina Mongelli told police. "He was also a cat burglar, breaking into houses at night to support our family, but he has never done any of these disgusting things."

Upon his arrest, police took Michele to hospital due to illness and his diabetes. Pietro Forno, Italy's top investigator into child sexual offences, led the state's prosecution. "I've dealt with many incest cases but this is the worst I have ever seen," he said.

The court found Lucia had been used for her father's satisfaction. She had been constantly detained and monitored, to prevent her from having contact with people who may recognise the abuse.

On May 23, 2010, Michele was sentenced to ten years

imprisonment, and Giuseppe was sentenced to nine years.

The family united against Lucia and brought civil proceedings against her. The family described Lucia as a "black sheep."

"That woman has a natural tendency to lie. She reported having been sexually abused, but in reality it was not so. She also says she was locked up in the house for twenty-five years, but enjoyed the freedom and could come and go from our home at any time."

In court psychiatrist Giorgio D'Allio testified, "[Lucia was] the victim of psychological slavery."

AFTERMATH

The family appeared across several Italian news outlets, after the media was invited to the Mongelli home, where they declared the innocence of their family members. Lucia's siblings defended their father and still respected him as an authoritative figure.

Michele's other son, Carmine, appeared in a newspaper after the arrests. He sported a fresh tattoo of his father's face, surrounded by crudely drawn stars and a wreath bearing the name "Michele." He stated, "I have always kept my father in my heart and here on my arm."

Caterina Mongelli denied the allegations presented against her husband. "None of this is true. It's all lies. My husband is in jail for something he didn't do. He only kept her inside because he was worried about her. Any father would do the same."

Lucia and Giuseppe's four daughters were placed under psychological care in a shelter. Lucia received treatment for a personality disorder brought on by the stress of her ordeal.

On November 18, 2010, Michele made an application to have his sentence commuted to home-detention. Mongelli argued that his health was "incompatible with the prison regime." The judge approved the application and he was released from prison. An appeal to the Supreme Court in June 2012 saw a warrant issued to have Michele returned to prison.

CHAPTER 23

JAYCEE DUGARD

ANTIOCH, CALIFORNIA — UNITED STATES.

2009

In Antioch, California — a city of around 100,000 people situated on the Sacramento-San Joaquin River Delta in Northern California — a young mother was discovered living in a backyard with her two children. A dirty tent was their home. They survived in squalid conditions, the backyard strewn with decrepit sheds and rubbish. On a tree branch near the tent hung a sign that read, "Welcome."

LEAD UP TO CRIME

Phillip Craig Garrido was 21-years-old when he started his career as a sexual predator. In 1972 he drugged and repeatedly raped a 14-year-old girl. He was arrested, but the case was dropped when the victim became too afraid to testify.

In 1976 Garrido kidnapped Katie Callaway Hall from South Lake Tahoe, California. He bound her and drove across the state boarder to Reno, Nevada. He raped her in a storage shed for eight hours, before police investigating a broken lock on the shed freed the woman. He was sentenced to 50 years in prison for kidnapping and 5 years for rape.

Garrido met Nancy Bocanegra, a nursing aid, while she visited her uncle in prison, and the pair married inside the prison walls in 1981. Phillip Garrido was released in 1988 after serving only 11 years. Despite being classified as a serious sex offender, he was released and returned to Antioch to live with Nancy.

Garrido was a musician who believed he would soon land a recording contract with a major label. He suffered delusions of religious grandeur, exacerbated by his use of narcotics like cocaine, LSD, and methamphetamine. He parked by schools, masturbating as he watched female students. Nancy would videotape him singing beside children's playgrounds, stalking and recording small girls at play. Believing he was an evangelist, he claimed he heard voices of demon-angels in the walls who would call for him to save the world.

Despite parole requirements that Federal officers monitor him, and his need for psychiatric care, Phillip Garrido was able to manipulate the system and those in authority.

In their backyard the Garrido's constructed a series of sheds on the ramshackle and rubbish-filled property. Nancy went scouting for a prize catch to give her husband as a gift. In her husband's old hunting ground of South Lake Tahoe, she spotted an 11-year-old girl.

HELD CAPTIVE

On June 10, 1991, Jaycee Dugard was walking to catch the school bus when Phillip and Nancy Garrido pulled their car up along side the child. Phillip shot her with a stun gun, dragged her into the car, where Nancy sat on top of her in the back seat as they fled. Jaycee's stepfather watched helplessly in the distance as she was abducted. He pursued the kidnappers on a bike but he couldn't catch them.

The Garrido's drove to their home at 1554 Walnut Avenue, Antioch — 256 kilometres (159 miles) from the abduction sight. Phillip forced Jaycee into the shower where he shaved what little body hair she had, handcuffed her, and then locked her in a shed in the backyard. A week later, when Garrido brought Jaycee a milkshake, he raped her for the first time. As time passed Jaycee became desperate for attention and human contact. She adapted to enjoy her captor's company, but would mentally distance herself while being abused.

Phillip Garrido would give her kittens and she wrote a journal about her love for her pets. He would soon take the kittens away and kill them. Jaycee wrote her name on her journal, which Phillip saw, sending him into a fit of rage. Afterwards, she was forbidden to say her own name and eventually took on the name of Alyssa.

The list of abuse was extensive. Garrido went on meth-fuelled binges he called "runs," where he would sexually abuse Jaycee and make her listen for hours to the voices in the walls. He often videotaped the humiliating abuse. The couple also recorded other young girls they scouted.

When Jaycee was 13 years old the Garrido's told her they thought she was pregnant. On August 18, 1994, she gave birth to a daughter, followed by a second girl on November 13, 1997. Jaycee learnt to take care of her children from watching television. When the girls were still young, Jaycee was moved into a tent in a fenced off section of the backyard. She set up a makeshift school for her daughters, teaching them reading, writing, mathematics, and social studies.

Nancy Garrido had no children of her own, suffering from a series of miscarriages. She grew resentful that the children addressed Jaycee as their mother. Still young enough that they would eventually forget, the children grew up believing Nancy was their mother and Jaycee was their sister.

Jaycee stayed in the backyard, never finding the strength to leave, being told by Phillip Garrido that the world was populated with paedophiles and rapists, and that her kids would not be safe if they left.

Towards the end of their captivity, the Garrido's would take Jaycee and the girls on family outings to carnivals and to neighbourhood parties.

RESCUE

Parole officers visited Phillip Garrido's house on more than 60 occasions, but never ventured into the backyard to investigate the series of sheds. On one occasion, Jaycee was in the house as parole officers searched it. She spoke to them, before officers drug tested Phillip and left. Phillip Garrido badgered parole officers with spitfire questions, while Nancy Garrido chased after them with a video camera until the officers left in frustration.

A neighbour reported to 911 that children were living in the Garrido's backyard. The neighbour said Garrido was "psychotic, with a sexual addiction." The local Sheriff investigated, but didn't look in the fenced off section of the backyard. Systemic oversights from parole officers and local police ensured Jaycee was not rescued earlier; this included Phillip Garrido taking his daughters along with him when he visited the FBI, submitting a manifesto detailing his cures for schizophrenia and unwanted sexual desires.

Campus police officers noticed Garrido while he visited the University of California, Berkley, on August 24, 2009. He was attempting to organise an event to promote his newly registered church "God's Desires." Officers sensed something was not right. The eldest girl clung to his side, staring at Garrido with unflinching admiration. When questioned, both girls spoke in a robotic manner. Officers ran checks and discovered Garrido had a history of rape and kidnapping.

Parole officers arrested Garrido, but again never searched the backyard and released him a few hours later. He believed angels guided him safe passage through his crimes. On August 26 he visited his parole office to discuss the Berkley visit, taking Jaycee and the girls with him. Through questioning, Garrido admitted to kidnapping and raping Dugard. In a separate room, Jaycee denied her identity, claiming she was a battered wife from Minnesota. She was detained. Then after 18 years of captivity, she was coaxed by an officer to write her real name on a piece of paper. The truth had escaped. She was finally free.

The California Department of Corrections and Rehabilitation Parole Division appeared on live television claiming credit for solving the Dugard case, which led to heavy criticism from the enraged public once the story broke of their constant failings.

TRIAL

After their arrest, Phillip and Nancy Garrido originally pleaded not guilty to the charges against them, as they attempted to setup their defence so they could plead insanity. On April 28, 2011, the case went to trial and the pair pleaded guilty.

Jaycee did not attend court; instead her mother read a statement on her behalf.

"I chose not to be here today because I refuse to waste another second of my life in your presence. ... Everything you have ever done to me has been wrong, and someday I hope you can see that. What you and Nancy did was reprehensible. You always justified everything to suit yourself, but the reality is and always has been that to make someone else suffer for your inability to control yourself, and for you, Nancy, to facilitate his behaviour and trick young girls for his pleasure, is evil. ... You do not matter any more."

Phillip Garrido was sentenced to 431 years imprisonment for kidnapping, rape, and false imprisonment. He is currently held at California State Prison, Corcoran; where Charles Manson is also held. He will never be released.

Nancy was sentenced to 36 years to life for the same charges as her husband. At the time of sentencing she was 55 years old. Her earliest current released date is in 2066, she will be 91. She is held at Central California Women's

Facility, Chowchilla.

AFTERMATH

Jaycee was reunited with her mother and she continues to care for her two daughters. She works with a therapist to assist with the reunification of the family and to help her adjust to her life of freedom. Jaycee and her children have had to adapt to daily life, and have had to deal with receiving unwanted attention from the media and the public.

Both Jaycee's daughters were unaware their mother had been kidnapped, or that they were being held captive, as Jaycee never told them. They were told the truth of their circumstances two days after their rescue. Her daughters attend school, where they are reported to do well.

The Dugard family reached a $20 million settlement with the State of California for neglecting to adequately monitor Garrido while he was a Federal parolee. Further legal cases are expected to commence against Government organisations by the Dugard family, continuing their fight for systemic change by the Department of Justice in how they manage offenders, especially sex offenders released into the community.

Jaycee wrote a memoir about her time in captivity: *A Stolen Life*.

CHAPTER 24

DUSTIN LaFORTUNE

REGINA, SASKATCHEWAN – CANADA.

2010

Dustin LaFortune was a handsome young man, who set out from the Canadian capital of Winnipeg to build a new life for himself. When his loved ones saw him next Dustin was almost unrecognisable, after having faced an ordeal that would leave him changed in every possible way. His hopes for the future would be torn asunder by a friend, who was also named Dustin.

LEAD UP TO CRIME

Dustin Paxton, 30, had been on the police radar since his teens. His father placed him in the care of social services when he was 12, disowning him and his bad behaviour. He quickly became involved in drugs and alcohol, establishing a juvenile record. In 2007 he appeared on Canada's Crime Stoppers Most Wanted list, and he had a criminal history of credit card fraud.

"He was in jail, in and out, in Winnipeg, in Regina, in Calgary — he was always in trouble," Paxton's aunt told a Canadian newspaper.

Dustin LaFortune grew up in Winnipeg as part of a large family, free from the influences of television, sugar, and violence. He had been in a four-year relationship with Lindsay Airhart, which resulted in one child. After they broke up the pair remained friends, living with each other for a further two years. Dustin LaFortune, a lumberyard foreman and weightlifter, decided to set out for a new life by travelling 1,300 kilometres (808 miles) from Winnipeg to Calgary. He joined up with acquaintance Dustin Paxton, who he had met three years earlier.

The two Dustins soon became roommates and worked together to establish their furniture moving business, Two Guys and a Truck. The business was registered to 4203 Centre Street Northwest, in Calgary, where a motley crew of friends also gathered regularly to drink, and smoke marijuana and crystal meth.

Paxton began abusing LaFortune in October 2008. The abuse started when LaFortune backed up a chair against an extension cord. Paxton reacted by hitting LaFortune in the head with a steel capped boot for ten to 15 minutes. He apologised the next day. Neighbours noticed LaFortune's face was swollen, resembling a grapefruit.

Abraham Chutta, 19, also worked for Paxton and shared the Centre Street house for a short period. Paxton's abuse against Chutta started with arguing, which escalated to slapping, then punching, to being hit with a police baton and whipped with a dog leash. Abraham was dragged from his room, forced to sit on the couch with LaFortune, as Paxton beat the pair.

"He held a knife to me and said if I ever tried to leave he would kill my family," said Chutta. He fled in 2009 but refused to press charges at the time.

During his stay in Calgary, LaFortune's ex-girlfriend, Lindsay Airhart, visited him. She described how Paxton controlled LaFortune and allowed him to eat only one meal a day. She asked him to leave with her, but he refused.

In September 2009, LaFortune was admitted to hospital in Calgary suffering from broken ribs, allegedly caused by a freezer falling on him. Once released, LaFortune became impossible to find, his phone and emails went unanswered.

In February 2010 a seven-minute phone call was made to 911, reporting an assault taking place at the Centre

Street premises. No police were dispatched after the 911 call-centre, operated by the City of Calgary, received the call. Other calls were made in January and April of 2010.

Dustin LaFortune's family first reported him missing on February 28, 2010, but were told their missing persons report didn't warrant an investigation. In early March, Airhart's father received a phone call. "He sounded like death."

HELD CAPTIVE

In early 2010 the pair travelled to Regina, the capital city of the Saskatchewan Province in Canada's mid-south — a city with a booming economy due to the oil industry, and surrounded by rich prairies that support agriculture.

Paxton and LaFortune moved into a three-storey brown brick apartment building named Elmwood Manor, at 2158 Halifax Street, Regina.

Neighbours didn't see the pair, and weren't even certain of who was living in the apartment rented in LaFortune's name, but they did hear a great deal. A down stairs neighbour reported hearing low distressed groans each morning, which escalated into the sounds of one-sided fights. He would hear screaming, and a male yelling such things as, "Open your eyes," followed by violent noises. When neighbours complained, Paxton threatened them with violence.

Over the course of 18-months, in Calgary and Regina,

Paxton had victimised LaFortune, beating him daily, often with a whip or bamboo cane. LaFortune was held captive, choked unconscious, thrown through drywalls and down stairs, and suffered sustained sexual assaults. LaFortune was forced to perform sex acts on Paxton to avoid physical abuse. A section of flesh on LaFortune's leg died from being repeatedly whipped.

Lindsay Airhart received a text message stating LaFortune was on a farm in Leduc, Alberta, and had no phone access. It was believed Paxton sent the text message, during the same period as he ensured LaFortune was incapable of leaving the Halifax Street address for over two months.

Dustin LaFortune failed to attend his cousins wedding, increasing the concern of his family. He appeared in public two days later, bearing little resemblance to the young man anyone once knew.

RELEASE

A man claiming to be LaFortune's cousin brought Dustin, now 26, to the Regina General Hospital on the morning of April 16, 2010. LaFortune's injuries were extensive; he was not expected to live and was placed on life support. He was emaciated, weighing only 41 kilograms, down from 113 (90 pounds from 250). His body was covered in lacerations, burns, and bruises. His ribs were broken, along with his skull. His face had been beaten and mutilated beyond recognition, his bottom lip cut off, his tongue missing, and his eye orbits broken. LaFortune displayed obvious signs of an acquired brain injury.

It took a month before LaFortune could speak. The injuries were so severe that LaFortune had trouble remembering what had happened to him. As he recovered the horrific memories came flooding back. "I just remember everything now," he said.

LaFortune stated that he didn't leave earlier as he was afraid of being perceived as a "sissy," because of intense fear, and because the brain injury he received from Paxton clouded his thinking.

"He was such a scary guy," LaFortune said about Paxton. "And so manipulative."

The hospital drop-off was caught on security camera. The manhunt was on for Dustin Paxton.

TRIAL

Paxton was arrested in Edmonton, Alberta, on August 22, 2010. Police launched a raid on the bungalow he was renting, sending in the tactical unit and the Fugitive Apprehension Sheriff Support Team.

He was charged with two counts of aggravated assault and one count of forcible confinement. Paxton was also charged with the unlawful confinement of an ex-girlfriend, dating back to 2001.

Regina police and the court went to great lengths to

keep details of the case suppressed, although many details were already published on the internet.

Paxton's trial began on September 27, 2010. He smirked in court as the charges were read against him. The trial was scheduled to last for five weeks, but lasted four months.

Paxton was found guilty of aggravated and sexual assault, but found not guilty of unlawful confinement. The court believed LaFortune could have escaped if he wanted. Justice Sheilah Martin read that the court understood "why Dustin LaFortune didn't leave, but there is a difference . . . between domination and confinement."

Paxton was also found guilty of uttering threats and assault with a weapon against Abraham Chutta.

Paxton was ordered to undergo further psychological evaluation, and undergo a "dangerous offender hearing" that could see him imprisoned indefinitely. The trial is due to commence on July 15, 2013, and should last four weeks.

AFTERMATH

Dustin LaFortune will require many more operations, including reconstructive surgery to his face, therapy for his acquired brain injury, and long-term psychological assistance.

"I still think the same about humans — that humans are capable of everything good. They're also capable of everything bad, too. You've just got to be smart enough to figure out one from the other," said LaFortune.

Because of his appearance Dustin waited before seeing his daughter, careful to make sure she was psychologically prepared to see him. The family engaged the help of social workers and trauma counsellors before the reunion. He continues rehabilitation under the care of his family and doctors in Victoria, Canada, at Victoria General Hospital. When returning home Dustin stated his aims included attending college and one day owning another business.

On February 1, 2012, the LaFortune family requested the media respect their privacy.

CHAPTER 25

LINDA ANN WESTON

PHILADELPHIA, PENNSYLVANIA

- UNITED STATES.

2011

A three-decade reign of terror spread throughout Philadelphia. Only briefly contained, the enterprise stretched its way across four states, collecting co-conspirators and victims as it grew. Standing in the centre of the complicated web, and the multitude of tangled lives, was the domineering matriarch Linda Ann Weston.

LEAD UP TO CRIME

Linda Ann Weston was released from prison on parole in 1987. She served a total of four years inside for the third-degree murder of her sister's boyfriend, Bernardo Ramos. Linda and her sister, Venus, locked Ramos in a closet and starved him to death. His body was dumped in a disused convent in Philadelphia.

Free to pursue a normal life, Weston became involved with Gregory Thomas; a man of low cognitive function who heard voices in the walls, a convicted rapist, and a former professional boxer. Together, they had four children in quick succession — Gregory Junior, Sophia, Shayanna, and Demetrius.

In 1990, Weston petitioned for custody of the four children she gave birth to by Peppi McIntosh before her incarceration — Jean, James, Joseph, and Raymond. James and Joseph had been living with their aunt since Linda Weston's 1983 arrest, but they were being abused while in care. They were locked in closets, beaten, forced to search for food scraps in the trash, and had cockroaches placed in their food. The children wanted to live with their mother to escape the abuse. The Family Court of Pennsylvania for Philadelphia County released the three eldest children into Weston's custody, an agreement arranged by a DHS caseworker who knew of her criminal background. The children were sent to live with their half-siblings, unaware of their mother's history. The youngest child, Raymond, was sent to live with an uncle.

The family lived in Frankford, Philadelphia, but Weston was unable to feed her children. She forced them to steal food from stores, and locked them in closets and the basement. The eldest child, Jean McIntosh, complied with their mother's orders to control the younger children, faced with being chained up in the basement if she refused.

HELD CAPTIVE

Joseph McIntosh was drugged and locked in a basement by his mother for over a year, missing an entire school grade. Linda Weston feared he would run away, after already making several attempts, and that she would no longer receive welfare payments for him. She claimed the boy she tormented was "basically psychotic"; an excuse she used when teachers asked about the abuse at home, and to have Joseph committed to the Eastern Pennsylvania Psychiatric Institute in an attempt to collect additional Social Security payments. He was soon found of sound mind and released.

Joseph escaped from his basement life on July 4, 1998, when he was 16. He was unchained and ordered to do the washing. As he went to hang it on the clothesline, he jumped the fence, never to return to his mother's house.

By autumn 2001, Weston began amassing her next collection of victims. She offered them a place to stay and companionship, while all along her intention was to steal their Social Security cheques. She moved through at least four states — Texas, Virginia, Florida, and Pennsylvania — to avoid detection, adding new members to her "family" along the way.

Gregory Thomas Senior helped her contain the captives with threats and violence. He secured their many premises by installing locks on the windows and doors.

It is difficult to pin down the final tally of victims of the clandestine operation, but all appeared to have been family members or mentally disabled people collecting disability payments. Some would make it out alive; others would not.

Donna Spadea

Donna Marie Spadea, 59, was a local of Northeast Philadelphia, who suffered mental health problems and was admitted to mental hospitals on at least two occasions. Her criminal history included shoplifting, and her life was in a constant state of flux, always searching for a new place to call home. Shortly after being released from one of her hospital stays, Spadea met Linda Ann Weston and Gregory Thomas Senior near Frankford. In the spring of 2005, Spadea moved in with the pair at 2211 Glenview Street in Castor, Philadelphia.

Spadea collected $130 a week in disability benefits from Social Security, but soon Weston applied to become her "representative payee" to collect the money on her behalf. The mentally disabled woman would call Weston "Mom."

It is alleged Weston held Donna captive in the basement, feeding her food laced with drugs in order to sedate her.

Another woman was also held in the basement at the same time, according to relatives. Desperate for nourishment, the frail woman braved the stairs. Weston struck her with a wooden spoon.

"What are you doing up here? Get back downstairs," one of Weston's relatives reported Linda saying.

Spadea escaped from the basement, making her way across the front lawn of the town house wearing a frightened expression. Weston spotted her and chased her back into the basement. A relative witnessed the event, but Linda claimed the woman was incapable of looking after herself and she was caring for the "messed up" creature.

Donna Spadea died in Weston's care on June 26, 2005, her body found in the laundry. Before police were called Weston allegedly altered the crime scene, placing nine bottles of pills beside the body to give the appearance Spadea had died from a drug overdose.

The medical examiner ruled that Donna Spadea died of natural causes.

Maxine Lee

Maxine Lee, 39, grew up in West Philadelphia. Her mother described her as a jolly person who fell in with the wrong crowd. She was a former security guard who became largely itinerant and estranged from her family.

Lee began living with Weston in 2002. Initially the two women engaged in a romantic relationship. However, Weston soon began collecting Lee's disability cheques, and beat Maxine with sticks, bats, and hammers. They moved to various houses and across state lines, in order to avoid detection. It would be several years until Lee's family heard from her again.

Maxine Lee lived with the Weston family, and other mentally disabled captives, in Paintrock Drive, Killeen, Texas. Two other women living in the house were forced into prostitution. Lee was forced to live in the attic. She fell through the ceiling and was beaten by her captors as punishment.

On October 1, 2008, four women moved into a small white weatherboard house at 7435 Hooper Street in Norfolk, Virginia. Weston convinced the landlord she took care of the three disabled women. Neighbours, who only sighted her occasionally, never got to know Weston or any of the countless people living at the house.

Lee was locked in a cupboard under the kitchen sink, but managed to break through the door. As punishment, she was stripped naked and locked away in the attic, forced to sleep on fiberglass insulation. She was occasionally fed beans and rice laced with drugs, but mostly she was left to starve.

Maxine Lee died on November 14, 2008. Her body was moved from the attic and placed in a bedroom on a chair, to give the appearance she died while watching television. Her hair had fallen out and her feet had suffered serious trauma. Her death was ruled as natural causes, succumbing to bacterial meningitis and the wasting disease, cachexia.

The occupants fled the house a few hours after reporting the death, abandoning their possessions, and leaving the house in a rancid state. A stench permeated through the rubbished filled rooms, and the bathroom was something witnesses did not wish to describe. Thomas, Weston and her daughter, Jean McIntosh, transported the other captives back to Philadelphia. Police were unable to track down the occupants of the house, or determine where they might be headed to next.

In 2009 the Social Security Administration investigated Weston for continuing to collect Lee's benefits after her death. She was ordered to repay an amount less than $3,000.

Florida

By October 2010 Weston and her gang of captors were renting a house at 5307 Manning Avenue, Northwood, West Palm Beach, Florida. Seven children, three adults and one disabled person were known to live at the house, according to the landlord.

Failing to pay their utility bills, basic services were cut off in January 2011. Police were called to the house on numerous occasions, at least once because of prostitutes working in the vicinity, possibly Weston's victims. They were evicted on June 1, after leaving the house uninhabitable, removing windows, wiring and plumbing, and smearing human waste on the walls. They were still seen in the area of the Manning Avenue address after their eviction.

During their time in Florida, the enterprise rented several apartments around the West Palm Beach area, but always fell behind in payments. One captive, Tamara Breeden, was seen by neighbours after being dumped on the sidewalk each morning to sell dirty clothes. She had bloody lips, and burns and bruises on her face.

Weston also began a relationship with a Florida man, Nicklaus Woodard, 24, who went by the name "The Enforcer." He physically abused Breeden, punching and pistol-whipping her. He also used his gun to intimidate and constrain other captives, forcing Derwin McLemire to return at gunpoint after he attempted to escape. He was locked under the stairs and made to drink his own urine.

Neighbours witnessed numerous organised dog fights, violent confrontations between females, and drug dealing. Four dogs belonging to the group had to be euthanased, another two were abandoned in an apartment, and a pit bull was found dead after they vacated the premises.

Gregory Thomas Senior was arrested on July 4, 2011, for stealing a car in Northwood, with police finding Linda

Weston in the vehicle. He failed to appear in court in September. On the same day of his arrest, Benita Rodriguez, 15, went missing in Florida. She had played with the children living with Linda Weston, and was last seen with Gregory Thomas Junior, 17.

Philadelphia

Weston and her enterprise transported the victims across state lines to 4724 Longshore Avenue in Tacony, Philadelphia, arriving in early October 2011. One of the seven apartments in the building, a former neighbourhood cinema, was rented to her eldest daughter, Jean McIntosh, now 32.

Four mentally disabled adults were moved into a disused room in the sub-basement, measuring about four by 2.1 metres (13 x 7 feet). They were already malnourished, suffering from years of abuse; their bodies were a record of past tortures. They were locked in the dudgeon with three dogs, and used a metal bucket and glass jars as toilets.

Locked in the sub-basement were:

• Edwin Sanabria, 31, and Tamara Breeden, 29, who were high school sweethearts. Homeless, they met Weston in 2001. Tamara Breeden was reported missing in 2005. Philadelphia police closed her case. She gave birth to three children while she was held captive: two children aged two and five years and another was stillborn. Sanabria did not know he fathered the eldest child, known as "Little L." He was told she died at birth and the baby belonged to Weston, and would only later discover the truth after reading about the DNA results in the newspaper.

• Herbert Knowles, 40, who went missing from Norfolk, Virginia, in 2008 while Weston lived there. He was born with spastic diplegia, cerebral palsy, mental retardation and development disabilities. He disappeared after telling family members he was going to live with his girlfriend and her mother.

• Derwin McLemire, 41, met Weston while chatting on a "party line" when he lived in Florida, and was convinced to move in with the Weston family. While held captive he was deliberately set upon by a pit bull, which tore off a large section of his right ear. The left ear was left to hang, attached only by a small section of tissue.

RESCUE

On Saturday morning, October 15, 2011, building landlord Turgut Gozleveli, 71, noticed unusual activity around the premises. Tenants had alerted him of suspicious activity, and of people entering the basement at night. On inspection, he found light bulbs had gone missing from the basement and dog bowls had appeared. He questioned the residents if they were keeping animals, but no one admitted to doing so.

Down in the bowels of the building he discovered a

chain wrapped around a door handle. In a small room he discovered three barking dogs, and two people sleeping under filthy blankets. He believed he had squatters. He then noticed two more mentally disabled people being held captive; one in a sleeping bag, the other chained by his ankle to the broken boiler. The victims had the mental capacity of children, were severely malnourished, and were close to death. They had been trapped in the sub-basement for around two weeks.

Officers moved down the wooden stairs into the basement of the apartment building and into the sub-basement. The dank holding room was something depicted in a horror movie, with dirt floors and ancient crumbling brick walls from the original cellar on the site, all secured behind a heavy steel door. Copper pipes lined the walls, running from the decrepit boiler, and flimsy mattresses lined the ground. The smell of human waste strangled the air in the pitch-black room.

The captives were released and taken to the nearby Frankford Hospital.

The initial search of the Longshore Avenue premises turned up the identification of 50 people, causing police to fear Weston and her crew were involved in a larger human trafficking operation.

Linda Ann Weston, 51, Gregory Thomas Senior, 47, and Eddie "The Reverend Ed" Wright, 49, were arrested on Sunday October 16, 2011. They were held on $2.5 million

CAPTIVE HUMANS

bond apiece.

After the arrest of her mother, Jean McIntosh removed her cousin, Beatrice Weston, 19, from a closet where she had been imprisoned. Beatrice had been placed into Weston's custody at age eight, and then held captive for ten years. McIntosh initially lied to police, making them believe she was merely a witness. Beatrice was officially reported missing in 2009. She had been tortured, left covered in lesions and burn marks caused by hot spoons, and her skin was covered in a network of welts from being fired at with a pellet gun. She had also been starved, beaten with a bat, and she had old fractures. She had missed out on her schooling and forced into prostitution. Police were astounded that she was still alive, considering the extent of her injuries.

"I've never seen anything like this in a living person. It's remarkable that she is still alive. There is no penalty that is too harsh for the people that did this," said Police Commissioner Charles Ramsey.

Jean McIntosh was arrested on Wednesday, October 19, 2011. She was charged with kidnapping, conspiracy, false imprisonment, unlawful restraint, aggravated assault, simple assault, burglary and trespass. Her bail was set at $1 million.

Ten people, aged between two and 19, were found in the apartment. Eight were taken in to protective custody, including missing Florida teenager, Benita Rodriguez.

Nicklaus Larone "The Enforcer" Woodard was arrested in Florida on April 20, 2012, for carrying a concealed firearm.

TRIAL

The Federal indictment of the case was unsealed on Wednesday, January 23, 2013. It acknowledged Linda Ann Weston as the ringleader.

Linda Weston was indicted on 196 charges, including murder in aid of racketeering, hate crimes, sex trafficking, forced labour, theft, and 140 fraud charges. The federal hate crime law, known as the Matthew Shepard and James Byrd, Jr. Hate Crimes Prevention Act, was introduced after both men were murdered, the crimes motivated by their respective sexuality and race. The hate crimes charge makes history, the first time it has been used to bring charges against persons violating the rights of the disabled.

Linda Weston pleaded not guilty to all state charges, which were dropped as the Federal charges were announced.

U.S. Attorney Zane David Memeger described the case: "Shocking does not begin to describe the criminal allegations in this case, where victims were tied up and confined like zoo animals and treated like property akin to slaves."

Nicklaus Woodard, 26, was arrested in Florida on the same day the indictment was unsealed. He faces extradition.

The co-defendants, Jean McIntosh, Gregory Thomas Senior, Eddie Wright, and Nicklaus Woodard, all face Federal indictment charges.

Weston may face the death penalty.

At the time of writing a Federal Court date has not been set.

AFTERMATH

The four captives removed from the sub-basement were placed in a state run care facility, where they receive ongoing treatment.

"I want to stay here for good," said Tamara Breeden, appearing positive about her new life, despite her disfiguring injuries.

Derwin McLemire told reporters about what he thought of Weston: "That was real dirty of you. That was wrong."

Beatrice Weston made some physical recovery in hospital, but still suffers psychological trauma from her ordeal. In August 2012 she launched a civil case against the City of Philadelphia: for failing to prevent her abuse; for placing her in the care of Weston; and for failing to act on multiple complaints that she was being held in a basement.

Benita Rodriguez was reunited with her family and returned to Florida.

Joseph McIntosh managed to overcome his harsh upbringing, and works as an assistant manager at

McDonalds. He lives with his brother, James, who works as a truck driver. The pair applied for custody of the family members held by their mother.

The death of Linda Weston's mother, Alice Collier, who died in the 1970s of apparent natural causes related to kidney failure, was reopened to re-evaluate if she may have been the first victim of her daughter.

CHAPTER 26

THOMAS FISCHER

BARMBEK, HAMBURG — GERMANY.

2011

On a summer evening in 2011 Thomas Fischer realised a plan that was years in the making. His apartment housed explosives and a homemade torture chamber, and combined with his sadistic wish, Fischer was about to unleash a wave of terror. As his plans were about to come to fruition, a simple knock on the door would change everything.

LEAD UP TO CRIME

When neighbours enquired about Thomas Fischer, 30, installing a security camera above his front door and lacing the outside of the windows with heavy barbed wire, threaded through large eye screws, he told them it was to deter burglars, claiming his flat had been broken into on three occasions. Neighbours were getting their first glimpse into the world of a sadist on the edge.

Unemployed, Fischer earned money selling Nazi uniforms online. He also scoured markets and online sale sites, collecting weapons, including; a gun, a grenade, and medical equipment to use for torture.

Fischer, a gangly man with an un-styled wispy beard and thin pointed features, was described as a cold sadist who never smiled. He would regularly visit homeless people, buying them coffee and ogling women. He was a self-confessed virgin, who froze in fear if approached by a woman.

Thomas Fischer was cautious not to say anything about himself. He wore military jackets, and those who knew him could see he was mentally unstable. Often he would ask associates where he could buy items such as guns or dental equipment.

Fischer once presented a friend with a box containing a rabbit. "Please kill it for me," Fischer instructed. "I want to eat."

Inside Thomas Fischer's ground floor apartment the

kitchen was stocked with more than a ton-and-a-half of non-perishable food items, enough for the captor and victim to hold out for months. The premises contained a total of 113 fire extinguishers. Eight extinguishers had been converted into fertiliser bombs, constructed from plans sourced off the internet. The bombs were rigged throughout the two-room apartment, designed to detonate when he had completed his plan, or if he was captured.

The small room, with white concrete walls and florescent light, was decorated only with what Fischer needed to fulfil his fantasies. The small flat was not so much a residence, but rather an aboveground bunker to see out the End of Days.

A yellow phone box weighing more than 250 kilograms stood inside the room. Fischer had modified the phone box, insulating it with soundproofing, securing an outside lock, and rigging it with explosives. He had constructed his own DIY cell and torture chamber, waiting for someone to inhabit it. The large windows of the phone booth faced out to a desk, where multiple computers were hooked up. He could watch his victim, even while he was online, as though she was an exotic fish in an aquarium. On the back of the phone box was an old sticker that read, "SOS."

It is unclear where the phone box was purchased, but many are available on the German version of eBay for a few hundred euros.

HELD CAPTIVE

On August 19, 2011, Fischer set his plan into action.

Fischer selected his victim, a 26-year-old Israeli born woman studying in Germany. Fischer was an acquaintance of the woman, having been introduced to her through mutual friends the previous May. He became obsessed with the woman and stalked her, becoming increasingly consumed by the idea of "owning" her.

Fischer lived a life of social isolation, though he desired to have a family despite never having a relationship with a woman. His obsession with starting a family became sinister and overwhelming. He fell in love with his victim and on hearing that she was returning to Israel soon he enacted his plan.

On this Friday evening in summer, at approximately 7:45 p.m., Fischer knocked on the student's door. When she answered, he kidnapped her at gunpoint. He constrained her wrists in handcuffs and took her back to his apartment in the Barmbek district of Hamburg. Other reports claimed she was seized off the street.

As Fischer directed the terrified student through his flat, she was confronted with gynaecological instruments lying on benches. He had purchased a mannequin to practice on, training how to use needles and scalpels. Also in the apartment were a number of pregnancy tests and a blow up doll.

Part of Fischer's plan was to contain the woman in his

flat and impregnate her. He had collected fertility drugs, and planned to use the gynaecological equipment to help her get pregnant and deliver the baby.

Fate would intervene with a knock on the door. Fischer answered.

ESCAPE

The captivity lasted only two hours. Fischer forgot to lock the door of his beloved phone box torture chamber when he answered the apartment door. Still in handcuffs, the terrified woman escaped from the phone box at around 9:45 p.m.

Fischer had constructed heavy wooden barricades to place over the windows, held in place with large wooden beams. The same beams were also designed to hold the front door in place. Fischer never had time to install the last segments of his trap.

The woman plunged through the window, lacerating her skin as she passed through the thick mesh of criss-cross barbed wire. She fell to the bushes below and ran up the street screaming for help. Fischer pursued his victim, but she managed to out run him and took cover at a friend's house. Neighbours witnessed the event and alerted authorities.

Fischer returned to his flat and waited for the police to arrive. When they discovered him he was carrying a 9-millimetre handgun, a grenade, and refused to speak.

Police discovered homemade explosive materials in the basement and the area was evacuated. Video would later emerge of Fischer carrying dozens of fire extinguishers down to the basement, some of which were then turned into fertiliser bombs.

TRIAL

"My son was an honest boy; there has never been trouble with the police," said Thomas's father, Hans Fischer.

Police were already aware of Fischer — in 2009 he was investigated five times for stalking, though no charges were laid. He had previous failed attempts at meeting women, which also escalated to stalking. In 2003 he stalked German actress Eva Habermann, writing her letters and setting up a camp in her garden. Other previous charges against Fischer included assault and fraud.

Thomas Fischer's charges for his current crime included: taking a hostage, depriving a person of freedom, and explosives violations.

In April 2012, the charges against Fischer were dropped because he suffered from a severe psychiatric disorder, resulting in him not being responsible for his actions, and therefore unable to enter a plea. His defence lawyer agreed with the prosecution that Fischer needed help provided by the state. Thomas Fischer was sentenced to an indefinite term in a secure psychiatric hospital.

AFTERMATH

"My life was in danger but despite everything, I managed to escape," the victim told an Israeli newspaper, a few days after her ordeal. "Everything is behind me now. I am staying at the home of the Israeli family in Hamburg where I originally intended to be while taking a course. I will be back in Israel in a few days.

"A lot of the things that were published in the media were exaggerated. They made him out to be a sadist who wanted to attack me — that's not true. The same is true for the gynaecological devices found in his apartment. It was total embellishment."

German police confirmed gynaecological equipment was found in the apartment, though it was not reported that any had been used on the victim.

After her ordeal the victim returned to live in Israel. Fischer offered an apology to her and hoped that she would heal as a result of the trial.

CHAPTER 27

LI HAO

LUOYANG, HENAN PROVINCE – CHINA.

2011

Li Hao (李浩) managed to fool everyone around him. He led a secret life, starting a horrifying business in his basement that would shock China and stir controversy throughout the Chinese Communist Party. It wasn't only the victims he held captive that almost didn't escape, but the story itself was almost buried forever within China's heartland.

LEAD UP TO CRIME

Li Hao, 34, lived in Luoyang City in the Henan Provence in China's mid-east, with a population of 6.5 million. Li worked as a Civil Servant at the Administration of Quality and Technology Supervision Bureau as a part-time night gatekeeper. The contracted employee was known as easy-going, friendly, and hard working. Li was a college graduate, a former fireman in the army, and a member of the Chinese Communist Party. He lived in the highly populated area with his wife, 24, and eight-month-old son, in a worn out Government built apartment complex, constructed in the signature style of Mao's new China.

In 2008 Li Hao purchased one of the buildings many basement storerooms, accessible only by descending a narrow stairwell and passing through an iron-bar gate. In August 2009 Li began digging through the storeroom floor. He tunnelled for over a year, creating a 60 centimetre (23 ½ inch) wide chute through the floor that extended down four metres (13 feet). He constructed two secret chambers, covering 30-square-metres, concealed behind a series of seven doors. He carried the soil out in nylon bags during the middle of the night and dumped it around the complex.

From the storeroom he set up an internet webcam business. The filthy storeroom contained two vinyl chairs, a bed, a television, and a makeshift kitchen. Li used the storeroom as a second living area, telling his wife he had a second job as a janitor that required him to remain away for 15 days a month.

Li used his night-time employment as a cover while he trawled the local nightclubs and popular karaoke bars throughout the city. He flirted with hostesses, promising young women money if they returned to his home for sex. Taking the women into the basement, Li kidnapped them and held them captive as sex slaves in a crime that shocked the country.

HELD CAPTIVE

Li held six victims in his underground room for periods of between two-months and 21 months. The chambers were furnished with bowls for ablutions, beds, and computers with no internet access.

Once contained, the women were forced to call Li "husband" or "big brother." He would regularly beat and rape the women, subjecting them to horrific acts of violence. Li would spend up to 15 days a month with the women in his sex dungeon, hidden underground, while his wife thought he was at work.

Without natural light or ventilation, the room quickly became dank and the air turned rancid. He provided computers so the women could entertain themselves by playing computer games and watching videos.

Li devised methods to keep the women subdued. He forced them to fight each other for his entertainment, or beat them himself, and fed them only once every two days so they would remain weak.

When a captive known in the Chinese media by the name of Fang Fang showed disobedience, Li murdered her with the help of her fellow women. This was a display of power and a warning to the other women.

Li's hold over the women was so great that he created jealousy amongst the victims, so they would fight over who would have sex with him, turning on each other and becoming proud of their conquests, police reported. During these fights Li used a woman named by the press as Keke to kill another captive.

Li's motivation was to force the women to appear in live internet sex shows for his own profit. He would drag the girls up through the dirt tunnel into his basement to perform.

For the next stage of their captivity, Li decided to pimp the women out, allowing them a taste of freedom in return for having sex with clients and providing him with cash.

ESCAPE

Li watched over the women as he pimped them out. On the morning of September 3, 2011, a female known as Xiao Qing (Little Blue), 23, managed to flee and alert officers at the local police station.

When police ventured into the basement and accessed the tunnel, they heard the women call out cheerfully; "You finally come home, big brother." When the women realised it was not Li, but the police, they began to cry.

Below the ground police discovered four women, aged between 16 and 24, huddled in the corner. Police were unaware the women were missing.

When police liberated the four women they discovered the bodies of two other women buried in a shallow grave in the corner of the room. The four living victims were taken in for questioning by police and three were later released. Keke was arrested for murdering a fellow captive.

Even after their escape the women displayed loyalty to Li, defending him during police investigations.

AFTERMATH

Li visited his sister, where he confessed to his crimes and asked her for money. On September 6, 2011, Li was caught as he attempted to escape.

Li's wife was not involved in her husband's crimes and remained unaware he was keeping women captive. She believed he was working nightshifts and only learnt of the situation when police detained Li.

After Li's arrest he underwent state run testing to evaluate his mental condition. He faced charges of murder, rape, and illegal detention.

Such sexual related crimes are rare in China; most kidnappings involve captives being forced to perform physical labour. The case has caused much debate, focusing on a perceived moral decline throughout the country.

It was reported that journalist Xu Jiguang, who broke the story, was visited by two members of Luoyang Municipal Committee of the Chinese Communist Party and he was questioned over how he obtained his sources. Officials blocked further details of the case from being released by claiming information may violate "state secrets." Fearing for his safety, Xu posted on Twitter, "An unlawful cadre keeps sex slaves, what sort of a state secret can this behaviour be classified as?" He also posted a photograph of the two Party members who questioned him. He fled the province.

Public criticism over the "state secrets" claim quickly resulted in four police officers being suspended, and an apology offered by the Police Chief.

TRIAL

Luoyang Intermediate People's Court sentenced Li Hao to death on November 30, 2012, for the crimes of murder, rape, organised prostitution, illegal detention, and distributing pornography for profit.

Three victims were also convicted under Chinese law, relating to the two murders of their fellow captives. The main woman convicted was sentenced to three years imprisonment, while two other captives were placed on probation. The Court gave the women leniency because of the extreme circumstances, but they were denied independent legal representation.

Li Hao awaits execution, possibly by firing squad.

CHAPTER 28

JIMMY LEE DYKES

PINCKARD, ALABAMA - UNITED STATES.

2013

An Alabama man's mind was racked with paranoia, conspiracy theories, and a doomsday wish. He attempted to draw attention to his twisted ideals. A man feared by his neighbours for his extremist views, and plagued with delusions of a tyrannical government, Jimmy Lee Dykes took action to prove he was in control. He was anything but.

LEAD UP TO CRIME

Jimmy Lee Dykes, 65, was a retired truck driver and a Vietnam War-era veteran who served in the Navy between 1964-1969. He had lived in Florida, where in 1995 he drew the attention of police when he was arrested for improper exhibition of a weapon, but the charges were dropped. In 2000 he was arrested for possession of marijuana.

Dykes moved to his property on Sandy Lane, Pinckard near Midland City, Alabama around 2011. He lived in a camper trailer on the 1.5-acre property, which shares a road with Destiny Church, in the heart of America's bible belt. After purchasing the land he fenced the boundaries with barbed wire and cleared the trees.

Dykes quickly caused discord with his neighbours. He listened to a constant stream of right-wing radio, and rambled on about his political beliefs and disdain towards the government to anyone who would listen. Paranoid delusions, and all encompassing beliefs about his rights as a landowner, saw him threaten to shoot children who trespassed onto his land. He ran routine nightly patrols of the fence line, carrying a flashlight and a gun. When an arthritic dog wandered onto "his half of the road," he bludgeoned the pet with a metal pipe. It died a week later.

Dykes built an underground bunker out of plywood, sand, and cinderblocks. He was happy to show it off. According to neighbour Michael Creel, "He was bragging about it. He said, 'Come check it out'."

239

Digging into the night, Dykes spent several months constructing his bunker. Dykes allegedly buried a plastic pipe, running it from his bunker to the front gate of his property, so he could hear when people entered his land. He spent up to eight days underground testing the bunker, telling neighbours it was a storm shelter. He explained he came from an area ravaged by tornadoes, and his fear of the weather made him believe he should prepare for the worst. Tornadoes weren't coming, but another kind of storm was on its way.

Dykes was to appear before court on Wednesday, January 30, 2013, charged with menacing after firing shots at a neighbouring family. He accused his neighbour, Jimmy Davis, of damaging a homemade speed-hump he had constructed on their shared road, by driving over it with his pick-up truck. He fired shots at the family. The day before he was to appear in court he made alternative plans.

Dykes befriended the local school bus driver, offering him the use of a purpose built turning area on his property, to allow the bus to turn around on the narrow lane.

On Tuesday, January 29, 2013, Jimmy Dykes laid in wait for the school bus to arrive on its afternoon run. As it stopped, Dykes boarded the yellow school bus by pretending he was offering the driver home grown broccoli. Bus driver, Charles Albert Poland Jr., 66, protested as Dykes, armed with a gun, boarded the bus and demanded two children to take hostage. Poland stood up and blocked the aisle, placing himself as a barrier between the children. He received four bullets for his efforts, murdered in front of 21 school children.

Dykes fled the scene with just one child, Ethan Gilman, who had reportedly fainted. Scared children escaped through the rear emergency exit of the bus and ran down the road to hide behind the church.

The quiet rural area of around 2,300 residents, surrounded by cotton farms and peanut fields, was soon to explode in population as police vehicles, the FBI, helicopters, fire trucks, ambulances, and the media thundered towards Midland City.

HELD CAPTIVE

Dykes carried his young hostage up a series of steps made from cinderblocks and barricaded himself in his homemade shelter, which measured 1.8 metres by 2.4 metres (6 x 8 feet).

Dykes contacted 911 and alerted them to the situation he had created. Arial drones were deployed to survey the area before law enforcement entered the property.

Police communicated with Dykes through a ventilation pipe, which rose up 1.2 metres (4 feet) above the ground. Police dropped medication, colouring books, and a toy car down the PVC pipe for the five-year-old boy, who suffered from Asperger's Syndrome and ADHD. A video camera and listening device were covertly entered into the bunker. As FBI agents watched Dykes they noticed his behaviour was erratic, but he stayed within the boundaries of his delusions.

The known survivalist stocked up on food, blankets, and a heater; planning for a lengthy stay. He had reportedly fitted the bunker with electricity and running water. He also fitted two pipe bombs, one in the PVC pipe and the other inside the shelter. Police initially refused to say if Dykes had any demands, but officials claimed the boy was crying for his mother. Over the coming days police would give little information away as they negotiated with Dykes.

Dykes allowed the boy to watch television, play with toys, and even cooked him fried chicken. Besides any psychological trauma relating to the event, Dykes did not physically harm the child. On the fifth day of the siege police thanked Dykes for taking care of Ethan.

A possible motive behind Jimmy Lee Dykes' crime began to emerge. For a man who had spent a vast amount of energy isolating himself and warding off human contact, he wanted to launch himself into the public eye and appear on television. He had developed a grandiose vision of himself and during the initial stages of the negotiations he allegedly demanded a television reporter and cameraman, so he could share with the nation his views against the government and taxes. The FBI didn't comply with his demands; instead they promised they would try and provide him with a video camera to record his statements. FBI agents remained in constant negotiations with Dykes, attempting to coax him out of his bunker, hoping for a peaceful resolution.

RESCUE

The strain quickly took hold of Dykes, as fatigue tormented his unstable mind. His conversations with negotiators became rambling loops. As the situation stretched into its sixth day, the FBI feared "the child was in imminent danger," as agents observed an agitated Dykes pacing and carrying a gun.

The FBI Human Rescue Team made two replica bunkers from plywood, where they practiced how they would rescue the boy. One replica was used to practice blowing off the doors, while the other was used to train how to enter the bunker.

The easiest way to gain entry was to have Dykes open the bunker doors, and they would need to lure him to act. Playing on the captors desire to present his message to the world, FBI agents convinced Dykes they were dropping off supplies for him just outside the shelter door, including recording equipment and medication for Ethan. He took the bait. As he unlocked the door and reached out, two stun grenades were thrown inside.

At 3:12 p.m. on February 4, 2013, SWAT agents

stormed the bunker. The boy was covered with a bulletproof vest, and Dykes was shot. Ethan saw Dykes die.

Dykes "engaged in a fire fight with the SWAT agents," stated FBI special agent Jason Pack.

"The Army came in and shot the bad man," Ethan recalled to his mother.

An ambulance left the scene soon after.

"The subject is deceased," said FBI special agent in charge Steve Richardson. The coroner reported he had been shot multiple times.

Ethan was taken to hospital. The boy was reported as physically unharmed, and in a playful mood.

AFTERMATH

Ethan was released from hospital and celebrated his sixth birthday two days after his rescue.

Within days of being released Ethan's mother, Jennifer Kirkland, appeared with her son on the *Dr. Phil* show and in media appearances with the Governor of Alabama. Ethan appeared to be happy and playful, seemingly largely unaffected by his situation. Kirkland stated that Ethan had trouble sleeping and was thrashing during the night, and she had concerns about him going on another school bus.

The media appearances, especially on *Dr. Phil*, drew widespread public condemnation, with criticisms that Ethan Gilman and his circumstances were being exploited.

The bunker was excavated as authorities collected

evidence. It was soon demolished as it was classed as a biohazard.

Jimmy Lee Dykes never got to voice his reasons that inspired the ordeal, and police stated they might never know what motivated him. A relative collected his body and took the remains back to Florida.

ABOUT THE AUTHOR

David Phoebe is an Australian based author, living in
Melbourne. He has studied *Professional Writing and
Editing*, *Professional Screenwriting (Film, TV and Digital
Media)*, *Justice*, and *Criminal Justice Administration* at
RMIT University. He mainly writes true crime and young
adult fiction.

David has published articles in newspapers and magazine
throughout Australia. *Captive Humans* is his first full-
length book.

He works in the field of criminal justice and lives with his
rescued cat. He likes cats. A lot. He also likes cooking.

www.ingramcontent.com/pod-product-compliance
Lightning Source LLC
Chambersburg PA
CBHW060840280326
41934CB00007B/859